D0770998

The Care of Alloy Spars and Rigging

David Potter

The Care of Alloy Spars and Rigging

Charles Scribner's Sons
New York

First U.S. edition published by Charles Scribner's Sons, 1980

1 3 5 7 9 11 13 15 17 19 I/C 20 18 16 14 12 10 8 6 4 2

Printed in Great Britain
Library of Congress Catalog Card Number 80–50082
ISBN 0 229 11628 0

Contents

Acknowledgements

My thanks are given to the following companies for providing technical data contained in this book: Kemp Masts Ltd, Lewmar Marine Ltd, M S Gibb Ltd, Norseman Ropes Ltd, all of Great Britain, and Selden Masts AB of Sweden.

Iain McLuckie provided films, and developed and printed the majority of the photographs. My wife Barbara put up with–and translated–my scribblings, corrected my grammar and spelling, and typed the entire book. She has also brought me down to earth on several occasions when I started delving into too great a depth on some of the technical information, and she added many useful points which I would otherwise have overlooked or covered too quickly.

All the drawings and photographs (except where individual credit has been given) were prepared and taken by the author.

Any comparisons made between various rigs and fittings are strictly personal observations, and do not in any way reflect the policies or views of any of the above mentioned companies. I take full responsibility for any errors of fact or fancy which may be present in this text.

Introduction

The amount of time spent in carrying out practical maintenance on alloy spars and rigging is quite small. The relevant points could be contained in one chapter of this book, assuming that other factors, such as wear, abrasion, excessive loading, bad tuning and general misuse of the equipment, have not made extra work necessary. Experience has shown that the majority of maintenance and repair problems stem from one or a combination of any of the above points.

It is my intention to itemise the various fittings and rigging items that make up the complete rig package, and show the problems that can be associated with that fitting or item of gear and the correct way to use and maintain them. Spars and rigging will give years of trouble-free use providing they are of correct size and strength, are not subject to unfair treatment, and are used for the task for which they were originally intended. Because it is almost universally used these days, I have concentrated on stainless steel wire in preference to galvanised, which only gets a brief mention (as does rod rigging).

The technical data in this book is expressed in SI (Système International) units, which are used in the same way in all countries. For those of us less familiar with the terminology, most information is shown in imperial or metric units as well.

one

Mast Sections

In order that the reader may better understand this book I must start at the beginning, which is with the mast profile, or section, so as to illustrate the importance and differences between various mast sections. I will also show in simple form the meaning of such mast making jargon as moments of inertia and neutral axis.

Extrusions

Most alloy masts are made into their profile shape by the method called extrusion. This involves semi-molten metal being forced through a porthole die and rapidly cooled on emerging. To form a complex hollow section, the solid centre part of the die is attached to the main outer part by strips of steel called bridges. These are designed to allow the semi-molten alloy to flow round them and then fuse together again, forming a continuous circle or hollow section.

Neutral Axis

The neutral axis of a section is the line about which the areas of material on either side balance. This means that if you were to place a sample of section on a ruler, then the point at which the section balanced would be on the neutral axis. The dotted lines X and Y in fig. 3 illustrate the neutral axis.

Choosing the Right Section

The selection of a correct size and weight of section for a particular application is a complicated and technical problem that is best left to the mast maker. When seeking his advice, it is worth ensuring that he is given enough information to enable him to make a correct judgement.

It is not only the height of the rig, sail area, size and displacement of the yacht which is critical; he will also need to know the righting moment of the boat. The righting moment is effectively the stability of the yacht and is expressed in Newton metres, or foot pounds; the yacht designer will be able to provide this information. The strength of a section is its moment of inertia and is expressed in in^4 (inches to the fourth), or cm^4 (centimetres to the fourth); see typical mast maker's data-sheet, table 1. The moment of inertia is the area of the material that is distributed from the neutral axis, times the square of the distance it is positioned from that neutral axis. From this it can be clearly seen that the powerful element in this formula is the distance the material is positioned from the neutral axis, as this figure is squared in the calculation. It can be seen from table 1 and fig. 1 that a section that has thin walls, and is therefore light and large in physical dimensions, can have a greater moment of inertia than a section which is heavy, small in physical dimensions, with a thick mast wall. So when comparing mast sections, it is of little use

MAST SECTIONS

Description	Section Dimension	Moment of Inertia Ixx cm^4	Moment of Inertia Iyy cm^4	Wall Thickness	Weight kg/m	Bolt rope Groove Width	Sail Slide Number
Tolerance	± 1%	± 10%	± 10%	+ 10% − 5%	+ 20% − 0%	As listed	
PEAR	86/63	42	25	2.64 2.03	1.48	4 +.75 −0	1134
	101/70	67	36	2.54 2.16	1.67		
	114/76	104	48	2.29	1.93		
	127/91	150	90	2.64 2.29	2.35		
OVAL	126/85	156	75	2.48	2.26	4 +.75 −0.00	1134
	130/93	215	100	2.50	2.71		
	138/95	287	140	2.85	3.35	5.5 ±.75	1135
	155/104	385	179	3.05	3.51		
	170/115	563	239	3.10	4.02		
	177/124	725	345	3.40	4.75		
	189/132	956	458	3.70	5.73		
	206/139	1241	586	4.10	6.16		
	224/150	1775	830	4.50	7.31		
	239/162	2360	1120	4.85	8.76		
	276/185	3500	1650	5.00	9.70		
DELTA	109/88	125	80	2.5	2.38	4 +.75 −00	1134
	121/92	205	122	3.0	3.06		
	129/100	292	175	3.5	3.73	5.5 ±.75	1135
	137/113	385	233	3.9	4.18		
	146/112	407	278	4.4	4.71		

BOOM SECTIONS

Description	Section Dimension	Moment of Inertia Ixx cm^4	Moment of Inertia Iyy cm^4	Wall Thickness	Weight kg/m	Bolt rope Groove Width	Sail Slide Number
PEAR	70/57	19.5	13.5	2.03 1.63	0.94	4 +.75 −0	
	76/60	31	19	3.10 1.63	1.13		
ROUND	89/89	78	60.5	2.30	2.16	5.5 +.75 −0	
	100/100	132	105	2.64	2.56		
	113/113	189	148	2.64	2.84		
	127/127	298	236	3.10	3.60		
OVAL	85/58	50	23	2.00 2.5	1.53	4 +.75 −0	
	111/75	120	59	2.00	2.23	5.5 ±.75	
	128/90	222	108	2.50	2.79		
	162/115	450	250	2.50	3.84		
	185/130	800	400	2.60	4.50		

ALL MEASUREMENTS IN METRIC

SPINNAKER BOOMS AND JOCKEY POLES

Description	Section Dimension	Moment of Inertia cm^4	Wall Thickness	Weight kg/m
Tolerance	± 1%	± 10%	± 10%	+ 20% − 0
	48/48	7.6	2	.49
	60/60	15.4	2	.90
	72/72	29.9	2.2	1.24
	84/84	48	2.2	1.38
	96/96	72	2.2	1.58

SPREADERS

Description	Section Dimension	Moment of Inertia Ixx cm^4	Moment of Inertia Iyy cm^4	Wall Thickness	Weight kg/m
Tolerance	± 1%	± 10%	± 10%	± 10%	+ 20% − 0
	70	11	0.6	1.7 to 4.0	.69
	95	40	2.2	2 to 6	1.26
	117	97	4.5	2.25 to 8	1.89
	140	207	10	3 to 10	3.06

Table 1. Typical mast maker's data sheets

looking at weights and physical size alone, it is the moments of inertia that are the key to the correct section choice. The weight, of course, is important, as a light displacement boat will not be happy with a heavy spar, although a heavier displacement craft will not suffer unduly from the extra weight aloft resulting from carrying a smaller diameter

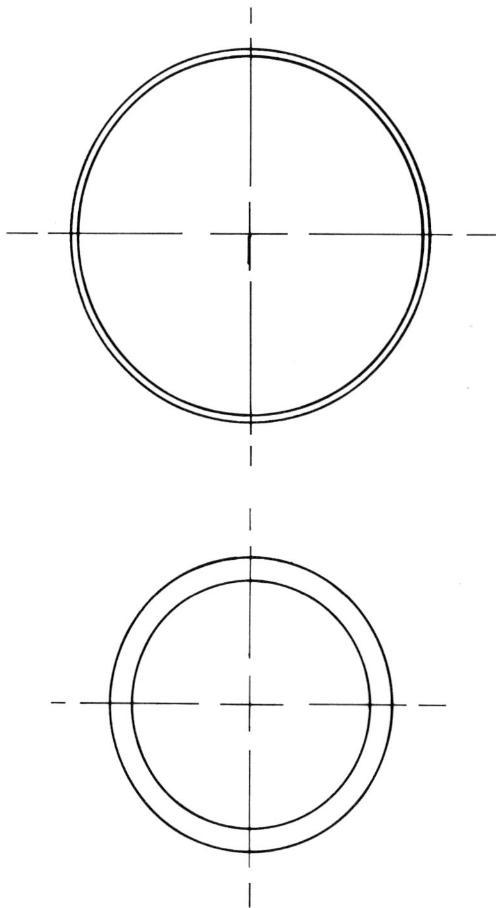

1. Section inertias. Top: a tube of 146mm outside diameter and 140mm inside diameter with a wall thickness of 3mm, a weight of 1·20 kgs per metre and an inertia of 347cm^4. Bottom: a tube with outside diameter of 120mm, inside diameter of 108mm, a wall thickness of 6mm with a weight of 2kgs per metre and an inertia of 347cm^4. When comparing them, it will be seen that both have the same inertias and are therefore suited to the same application, although they differ widely in physical dimensions and weight.

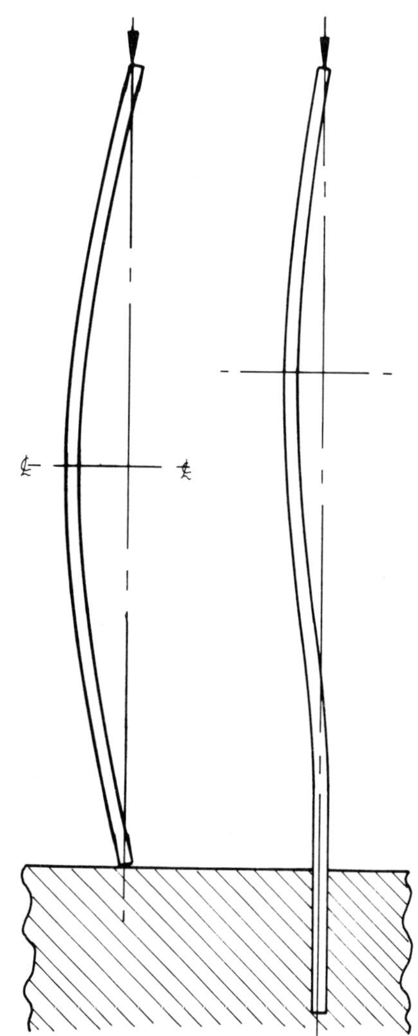

2. Two bamboo canes of equal length above ground. The one that is standing on the ground will bend uniformly with its greatest deflection in the centre. The one with 20% of its length in the ground will have less bend, with the maximum deflection at a higher point for the same load.

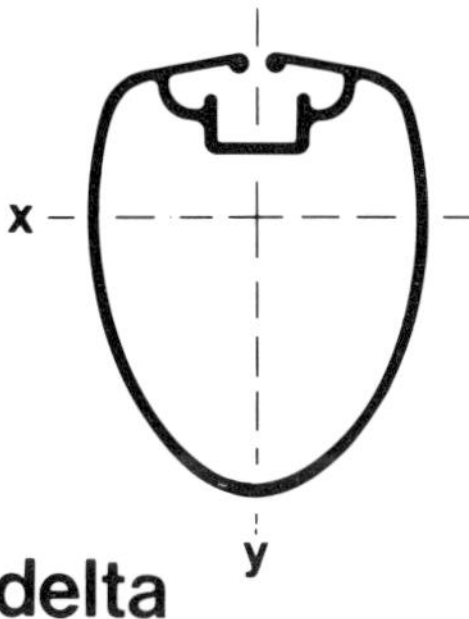

3. Dotted lines X and Y show neutral axes rather than centre lines. Line Y is also the centre line, as the section is symmetrical each side of this line.

mast. A yacht with fine bow sections will be less happy with a heavier mast, as the inertia of the rig will make the yacht pitch far more than a boat with fuller sections forward of the mast.

It is at this point that the reader may ask how is it that the moment of inertia relates to a given application. It is this figure that is put into the formula used for working out the load at which an unsupported panel of the mast will buckle (Euler formula). It will only be confusing to give the formula at this point, as there are several different forms of it, depending on the way the mast is stayed and supported. For instance, a deck-stepped mast has a different formula from a keel-stepped mast, as the keel-stepped mast gets extra support from the chocking of the deck partners. The easiest way to illustrate this point is with a bamboo cane. If this is made to stand on a solid surface, and hand pressure applied to the top of the cane, the cane would bend uniformly throughout its length, with its greatest area of deflection in the centre. On the other hand, if a cane 20 per cent longer were placed with the extra part of its length in the ground, making the two canes equal length above the ground, and the same pressure applied to the top, the second cane will bend at a much higher point and far less than the first example (fig. 2).

Practical Stability Test

When a mast maker does not have all the information on the stability (righting moment, fig. 4) of the boat, and therefore finds it difficult to calculate the loads in the rig, he may decide to do a practical stability test. This involves the yacht being inclined by pulling her down to an angle of heel of 30° (plate 1) by the use of blocks and tackles from the mast head; the load involved to heel the yacht is measured. This load is not at right angles to the mast head, so the reading must be corrected later, and to do this, the angle of pull has to be noted as well as the load and angle of heel of the yacht. As mentioned earlier, the angle of heel is normally taken as 30° because the stability of most yachts is linear up to 30°, but after this point the stability curve will start to fall off (fig. 5).

Plate 1. Inclination test on a 32ft yacht. The dial in the foreground is measuring the load to heel the yacht. The line from the top of the dial gauge is attached to the yacht's mast head.

Section Shape

There are three principal section shapes in commercial use today, the pear shape, oval and delta sections (fig. 6). There is little difference in windage between them and therefore the choice of section has to be made on other grounds. The oval and pear shaped sections both have inertia ratios of about two to one, whereas the delta section has a ratio

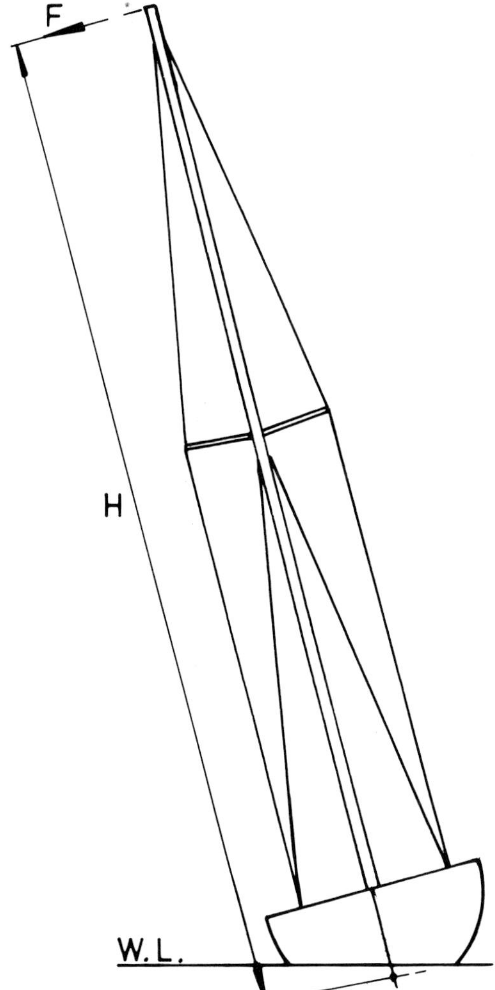

of about one and a half to one. It is these ratios which help selection. For example, the oval and pear shaped sections are better suited to masthead rigs, and the delta is ideal for three-quarter rigs, where greater fore and aft flexibility is desired. These points are very much a rule of thumb, as there are many other considerations which affect the choice of section and inertia ratios. The main consideration is the way in which the spar is

4. Righting moment: to calculate the compression loading in the mast it is essential to know the force F which makes the boat heel 30°. The height that this force is above the centre of buoyancy gives the second part of the formula which is righting moment=F×H.

5. Typical righting moment curve for a moderate displacement 10m (33ft) yacht. Note that stability is linear up to 30° (KN=Kilo Newtons).

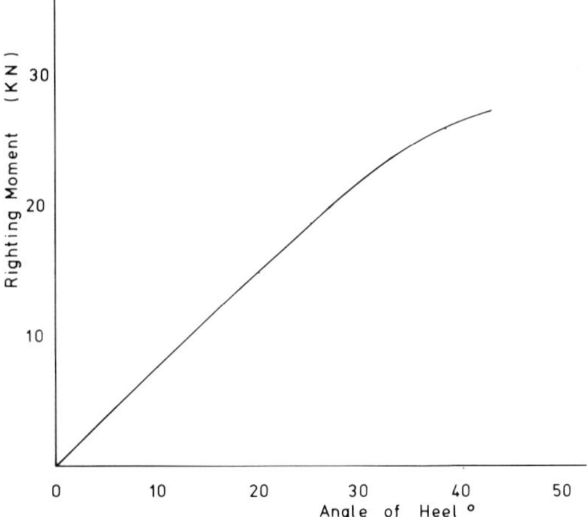

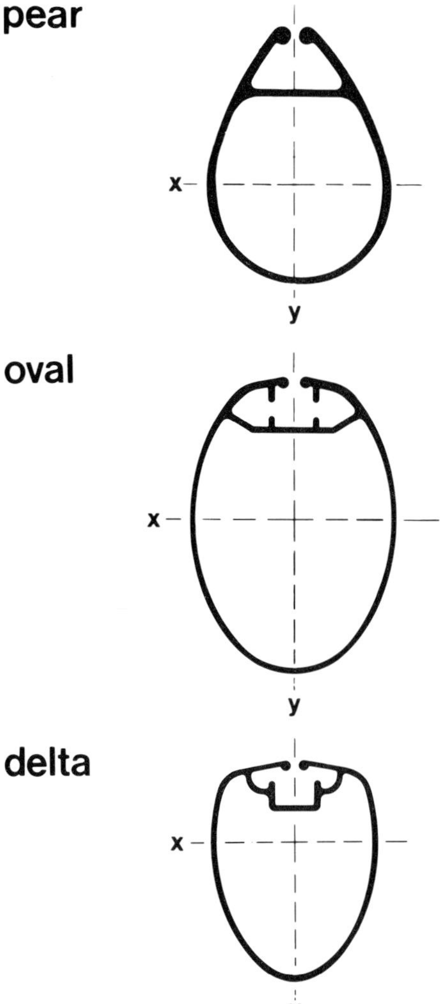

stayed. If a masthead rig were, for example, to have good fore and aft staying from the spreaders, a lower inertia ratio could be used. Chapter 3 will deal more thoroughly with staying arrangements, and I will go into more detail there. Another point to consider is the number of spreaders for which the rig is designed. A single-spreader rig splits the mast sideways into two panel lengths, but fore and aft it has less staying. If the forward and after lower shrouds are at an angle of at least 5° to the mast when viewed athwartships, then the mast is almost as well supported fore and aft as it is athwartships (the support angles are less), so you can use a section with an inertia ratio of 1·5 : 1. If the lowers are angled at less than 5°, a 2 : 1 ratio will be required. If the lowers were in line with the cap shrouds, you would require a section with a four or five to one inertia ratio, which is not available. In these cases, adjustable preventers are used on a 2 : 1 ratio section, but you will find that most mast makers are very much against such poor staying arrangements. If the mast were double-spreader rigged, the mast would be split into three panels athwartships and two fore and aft, so the 2 : 1 or even 2·5 : 1 ratio would be the best choice.

6. Mast sections: the three most popular and commercially available mast sections are the pear, oval and delta.

two
Mast Making

Anodising

By far the best protection that can be given to an alloy mast is for it to be anodised. The three commercial colours used by mast makers are silver, gold and black. The protection given to the alloy is exactly the same in all three cases, the colour being a dye used in the final process which in no way adds to the anodising protection. Mast makers favour silver anodising for several reasons. First, it is cheaper for the anodisers to produce a silver finish. Secondly, from the wear and tear point of view it is the most practical choice because scratches, abrasions and knocks do not show up so much, and the mast remains looking new for longer. Gold anodising will, in time, fade and will show up any scratches or handling marks which will appear during the life of the spar. The same is true of black anodising, but to a greater degree; any abrasions will show up prominently and the spar will lose its good looks. The black dye used in the process is the least colour- and light-fast of all, causing the spar to fade rapidly in sunlight. After one or two seasons, the spar will appear grey in colour. Spar makers therefore do not consider black anodising to be commercially favourable, and there is often a surcharge to the customer if a black finish is specified.

Anodising is an electrolytic process which makes the surface of the alloy impervious to corrosion. It can also give a harder finish, giving a little extra protection against abrasions. Anodising is not a protective layer on the surface of the alloy (as paint would be), it is a protective finish *within* the surface of the alloy, and is usually between twenty and twenty-five microns deep. A protection of less than fifteen microns is unsuitable for a marine environment; some anodising methods give only five to ten microns depth, and these should be avoided, even though they would be cheaper (see plate 3). Make sure you find out the specification before you commit yourself.

Any scratches, knocks or abrasions are difficult to treat cosmetically, and it is virtually impossible to match with paint the translucent effect of anodising. The best way to protect damaged areas, particularly scratches, is to polish the mast. On silver masts, the colour difference between the anodised area and the natural colour of the alloy is hardly noticeable, and protection is all that is required. If the damaged areas were to be left untreated, then they would corrode and turn grey in colour, showing up against the anodising of the mast. For colour anodised masts (black and gold) a paint touch-up is the only answer although, as stated earlier, a colour match is virtually impossible.

Both the inside and outside of the mast section are anodised, so the mast is protected from internal corrosion, and will not produce the grey deposits on internal halyards that will occur with masts treated by any other method.

Plate 2. A machine for polishing the mast before anodising.

Painting

Spars were painted long before anodising tanks were large enough to accommodate them, and with the improvement of paints and colours over the years, perhaps it seems surprising that so few spars are painted nowadays. However, painted spars will not resist abrasion damage as well as the hard anodised surfaces, because it is difficult to get the paint to key onto the alloy properly. Only when correct etching and priming is carried out under controlled conditions can any satisfactory form of adhesion be expected;

Plate 3. Corrosion on an unanodised sheave after one season's use.

painted surfaces may then approach the durability of anodising. However, scratches incurred during rigging, transportation and sailing can be easily and acceptably repaired with touch-up paint. Painted spars are not limited to new boats; if a yacht has old alloy spars, the chances are that they were painted or left in an untreated state, in which case they will be stained and pitted, and will leave grey deposits on the sails and halyards. Having these older spars coated can add resale value well beyond the cost of painting. Painted spars (apart from touching-up) will require repainting completely every four or five years, a maintenance chore that would not be necessary on anodised spars.

Painting spars is expensive, primarily because of the amount of labour involved. You can help keep the cost down if you prepare the spars for the paint shop by removing and labelling all rigging and mast fittings: a job that requires time and patience, although not necessarily expertise. A Sunday or two of your own time could see the spar undressed. It is, however, a waste of time for you to attempt to save money by preparing the alloy surface for painting. The preparation requires special materials and expertise, and is really best left to the professionals. As stated earlier, aluminium is one of the most difficult materials to paint, and only with extensive preparation will any coating adhere adequately. Aluminium corrodes (oxidises) in a short time when exposed to the air, and this superficial corrosion will severely inhibit the paint adhesion. The object is to provide a clean, oxidation-free surface to which the paint will bond.

The solution to the adhesion problem involves a multi-stage preparation process. The smooth, shiny extruded finish of a new mast is not a good surface for the paint to key onto: it must be roughened, and this is best achieved by acid etching through dipping the mast into an acid tank. The etching process provides a microscopically roughened surface to which the primer and undercoats will adhere. After etching, the acid must be cleaned off with hot water. The roughened surface can also be achieved by the amateur with special disc or vibration sanders, but the dust created by this method will lodge in the marks left by the sander, and will prove difficult to remove. It is difficult to tell how much dust is left on the prepared surface, and if any of this is not removed, it will cause blistering and adhesion problems for the painted finish; scrubbing and rinsing in hot water is the best answer.

Acceptable results are possible with sanding, but the acid etching process offers superior adhesion. Once the surface has been prepared and cleaned, as previously described, oxidation will begin immediately, and must be inhibited with a zinc chromate wash primer. This will etch itself into the surface and act to prevent further oxidation of the mast surface. The final preparation before the finished coat involves painting the spar with a two-part epoxy zinc chromate undercoat. The epoxy undercoat provides good adhesion to the alloy, and gives a surface to which the polyurethane can adhere. The epoxy undercoat gives a tough coating, and the zinc chromate further inhibits oxidation.

When the undercoat has cured, the spar will be ready for the final coating. No further surface preparation is needed unless the epoxy coating is left to cure for more than a day or so, when light sanding of the undercoated surface will be required for best results. The final polyurethane coat should be sprayed on, with the number of coats being dependent on the type of equipment and technique used. Properly sprayed, one or two coats will be sufficient for a durable and attractive finish. Application with a brush is possible, but the finish is inferior, because polyurethane has less tendency to flow and smooth out the marks left by the brush. Do not handle the spars after the final coat for at least thirty-six hours, and then only with extreme care, as the finish continues to cure for days, and even weeks, depending on humidity and temperature. The surface will not reach maximum hardness until it is fully cured. Polyurethane paints are relatively toxic and respirators should be used; where skin is sensitive, gloves must be worn, and all other parts of the body should be covered. Do the work in a well-ventilated area. All paint manufacturers' recommended safety precautions must be taken and all material instructions followed: leaving out or short-cutting any steps will result in an inferior coating or questionable durability, and paint spraying without a respirator can cause lung damage. The polyurethane paint finish on spars can be summarised as follows: pay a lot and you will get a lot, pay a little less and you will get a lot less.

Scratches

Scratches are readily repaired on painted spars. You should wipe off the surface of the scratches and clean them with the paint manufacturer's recommended solvent. Directly after this, apply paint with a small brush (a child's paintbrush is ideal). It may be desirable to thin the paint slightly, to help it bond with the solvent-softened paint surface. If the scrapes are large, follow the preparation methods for the original application. Painted spars can be washed with warm, lightly-soaped water. Cleaning with solvents is risky, as the gloss can be removed by some of the stronger solvents. Never use scouring pads.

Other Forms of Protection

A third possibility is not to use either of the above methods, but to purchase the spar un-anodised, and protect it with frequent coatings of wax polish. This will certainly help to protect the alloy, but the highly corrosive mixture of sea water and air will invariably make inroads. To a certain extent, the corrosion is self-inhibiting, and by this I mean that once the oxidised layer has formed on the surface of the mast, this itself provides a protective layer, so that the corrosion does not continue at the same rate beneath the surface. The oxidised surface is a problem, because it will cause black deposits on your hands, and will be transferred to your sails and ropes. The purchase of an unanodised spar is therefore only suitable as a short term solution, for instance on an experimental rig. As a long term investment, say for the family cruising man with a boat which will be owned for some years, professional anodising, despite the initial cost, is the only satisfactory and durable answer.

Welding

Yacht mast alloys are heat-treated, and therefore any welding activity will anneal the alloy, thus reducing its strength. The strength could only be regained if the metal were to be heat-treated again after the welding process. This would be a very expensive operation, and is not considered to be commercially viable. Annealing is heating the material, making it soft and ductile; alloys treated in this way will be approximately half as strong as the original material.

The welding-in of masthead fittings is acceptable, as these fittings are only in compression, and the softened areas are confined to the slot into which the head box is fitted, and thus the welding is spread over a large area. The practice of welding-in exit boxes at the lower end of the mast is acceptable, providing they are not placed close to any other fittings. If these boxes are at the base of the mast, they will be structurally sound, providing they have not removed more than half of the tube at that point. A welded masthead taper is perfectly acceptable as the weld runs vertically and it is in a low compression area of the spar (compression from the lower shrouds only affects the mast below the spreaders). From the above, it can be clearly seen that welding operations must be rigidly controlled or avoided completely. Areas where welding causes many mast failures are in the regions of high structural fatigue such as spreader brackets, shroud

Plate 4. Welding a mast taper. The welding of alloy spars is a skilled and carefully controlled operation. It should not be attempted by anyone without knowledge of alloys and mast structures.

tangs and any peripheral welds in way of the butt joint (a peripheral weld is one running around the spar instead of up and down it). Spreader brackets are subject to torsional loads imposed by the spreader outer end being held on the cap shroud so that the mast works fore and aft at the inner end of the spreader, thus imposing intermittent loading on the welded brackets which is far higher than the straight compression load through the spreader caused by the deflection of the cap shroud. This intermittent loading can cause fatigue in the welded areas round the bracket, so look out for the first telltale cracks appearing. Shroud tangs are subject to high fatigue due to the loading of shrouds as the yacht tacks, and the ever-present vibration that can be felt in the rigging wires, especially when sails are flapping or spilling wind. Fatigue will always find the weak link so if, for example, a tang has a welded doubler where the weld runs across it, this is one area in which the stress will first appear; any welding in or on the shroud tang should be avoided. Any peripheral welds or partially peripheral welds–for any reason–should be avoided, as this causes a weak line round the section just as a line of holes would, on the 'tear along the dotted line' principle.

The last danger area in welding operations is the welding of dissimilar materials i.e. the welding of an alloy casting to the mast section (extrusion). These alloys are completely different in their chemical, molecular and mechanical structures, and any welding of the two will only meet with partial success. If castings were to be used in conjunction with the three problem areas discussed above, I would label them as potential disaster areas.

Electrolytic Action of Dissimilar Materials

Stainless steel and aluminium alloy have an electrolytic action when oxygen is excluded. A zinc chromate paste should always be used between stainless steel fittings and the mast wall, for example stainless steel spreader brackets and shroud tang support plates. For this reason, you must be very careful when selecting the type of mast fastenings to be used. Any rivets should be alloy or monel: the use of stainless steel self-tapping screws should be kept to a minimum, as corrosion will also occur around these fastenings. Also, the points of the self-tapping screws penetrating the inside of the mast wall will cause snagging and tearing on internal rope halyards. Fittings such as metal cleats should have a pad of inert material separating them from the mast.

Sound Deadening

This term used by most mast makers is slightly misleading, as it is not possible to sound deaden alloy masts completely; it is only possible to minimise the noise from the slapping of the halyards on the inside of the mast. Any noise that occurs outside the mast has to be dealt with in the usual manner by tying the offending ropes away from the mast. Sound deadening will not help to solve this problem.

Many masts are sound deadened by the use of expanded polystyrene sheets which are rolled into cylinders and inserted as a continuous lining in the length of the mast. These linings are only 10mm or so thick, and do not hold the halyards very far away from the mast wall. It is because the sleeve is continuous that this method works. Another method is to use 150mm moulded polystyrene sleeves which have wall thicknesses of 25-35mm. Because these sleeves have such thick walls, they hold the halyards further away

Plate 5. Mast assembly lines.

from the mast wall, and because of this they are not used to form a continuous layer on the inside of the mast; they are positioned every two metres or so up the mast. The halyards would have to be left very slack for them to flap and reach the mast wall causing noise. Both these systems rely on the internal halyards being held, or guided, towards the centre of the mast. This means that at the bottom of the mast, exit boxes instead of exit slots must be used. If the halyards were to exit through slots, at that point they would be very close to the mast wall and any sound deadening material close to this point would be cut to shreds and be virtually useless after one hoisting. If large diameter sheaves are used at both the head and the heel, the halyards will be in the centre of the mast, and if good tension is kept on these halyards, there is little danger of them hitting the side of the mast wall. In this case sound deadening is an unnecessary luxury.

three

Setting Up and Tuning

The proper tuning of the rig is of great importance, so much so that it is often possible to support a weak mast profile with correct rigging, but a strong mast profile can fail due to improper and inadequate rigging.

Rigging

For single spreader rigs that are deck- or keel-stepped, the following information should be noted.

1. The compression load which the mast step must withstand is generally between 1·5 and 2·5 times the displacement weight of the boat.
2. The loaded stress which the stay fastening and chain plates must withstand is nearer to the displacement weight of the boat.
3. The chain plate for the upper shroud must be mounted on the mast adjacent to the mast centre line, or a maximum of 20mm aft of the mast centre line. It should never be forward of the line.
4. The vertical angle of the forward lower shrouds must be at least 5° from the mast centre line, viewed from abeam (see fig. 7). This requires that the distance of the lower shroud chain plates forward of the upper shroud chain plates shall be a minimum of 9cm for every metre of the vertical distance between the spreaders and the chain plates. It is particularly important that forward angle of the forward lower shroud is never less than 5° and, to fulfil this requirement, an inner forestay (babystay) is always acceptable. The after lower shroud angle is not so critical, and can be between 3° and 5° (see fig. 7).
5. All fastening points for shrouds and stays should be angled in the direction of pull.
6. The mast step must be fitted horizontally so that the mast cannot be loaded on the forward or aft edge of the mast (fig. 8).

The purpose of staying the mast is that it should stand straight when under sail. When rigging, give the upper shrouds and backstay a tension of 10 per cent of the yacht's displacement; this will result in a slightly higher tension on the forestay. After this, the forward lower shroud or babystay can be tightened so that the mast bends slightly forward at the spreaders. Next, tighten the aft lower shrouds: it is difficult to do this by hand. Tape all cotter pins and locking rings. The locking rings in the turnbuckles (bottlescrews) must be taped to prevent ropes catching on them and inadvertently opening them. The mast track must not deviate in straightness more than a maximum of one per cent of the mast height and, as soon as the yacht is under sail, the rigging must be adjusted to meet this requirement. Because many of the components in a rig will stretch a few millimetres when new, especially wire, it is not necessary to spend too much time attempting to stay the mast perfectly until the boat has been sailing a few hours with a maximum effective angle of heel. Only after this can effective setting up be carried out, and this is best done during moderate sailing winds (see fig. 9).

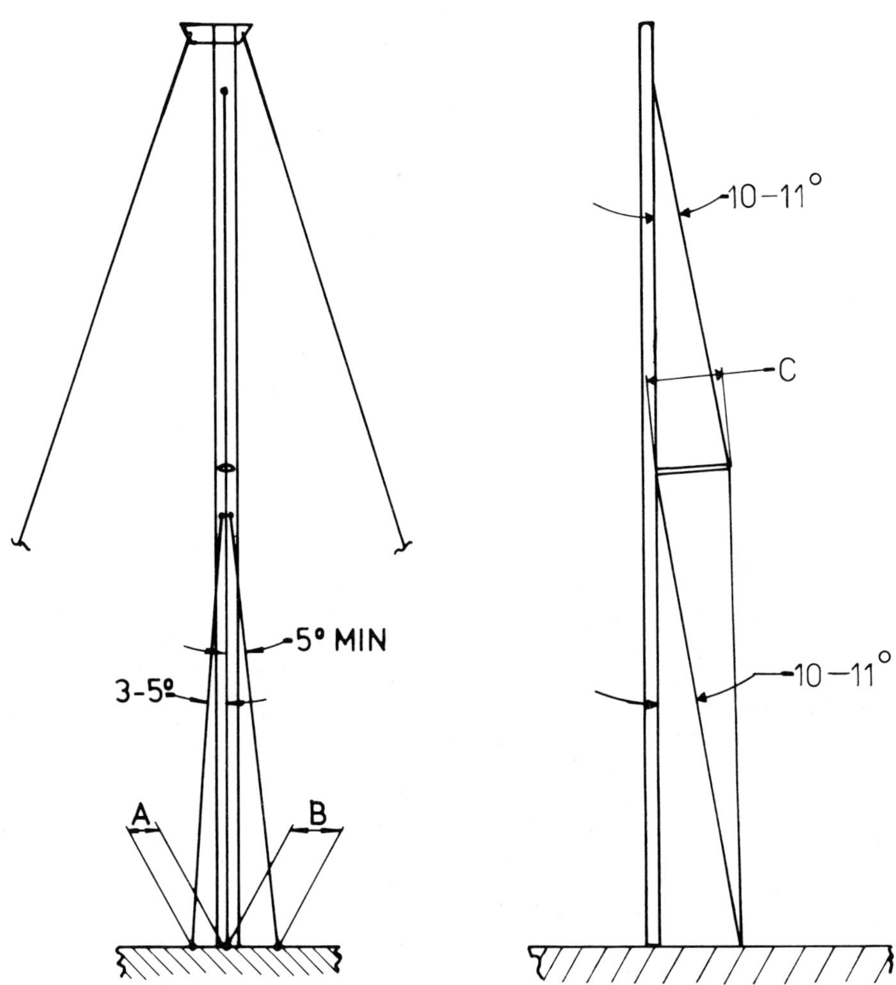

7. Shroud angles. Fore and aft: for a minimum of 5° forward shroud angle, dimension B should be 9cm for every metre of vertical distance from the spreaders to the deck. For the 3° to 5° after lower shroud angle, dimension A should be 5-9cm for every metre of vertical distance from the spreaders to the deck. Athwartships: the cap shrouds are on the athwartships mast centre line. For the 10° to 11° angle, dimension C should be 17·5-19·5cm for every metre of vertical distance from the spreaders to the deck.

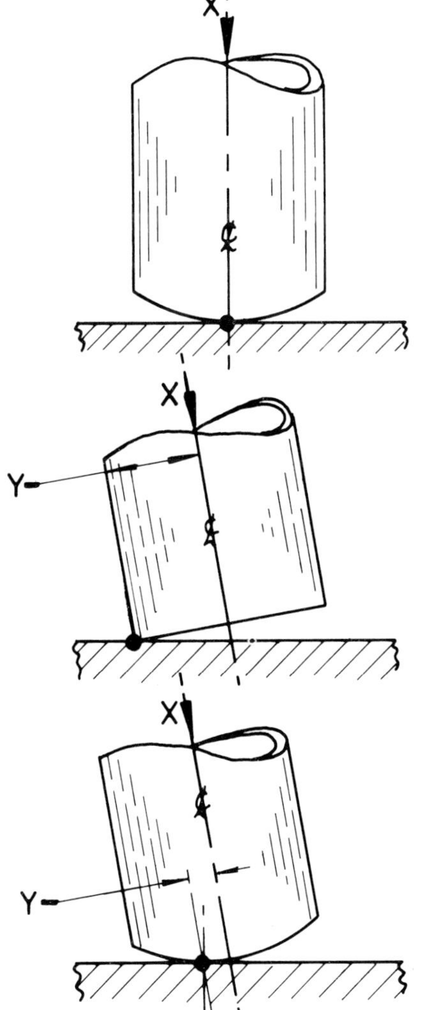

If the upper rig has been set up to the required 10 per cent of the yacht's displacement, the entire tuning can be done on the lower shrouds, so that the mast is straight both fore and aft as well as athwartships. The only possible deviation from the rule on the mast not bending by more than one per cent of the mast height is if the mast, when maintaining a straight line athwartships, has an even forward bow from the mast step to the mast head. This deviation can be as much as two per cent at the middle of the mast if the curve is controllable, that is to say, any additional bend or movement when the boat is thrashing to windward in heavy seas is unnoticeable. Should extra movement be observed, the lower shrouds must be adjusted to prevent this excess movement exceeding the two per cent permissible limit. It is mainly the inevitable stretching of the stays and shrouds that causes problems in the masthead rig. Rod rigging has twenty per cent less stretch than 1 × 19 stranded wire for the same diameter, but I do not advise it for general purposes because of a tendency to brittleness

8. Bending moments at the base of the mast. Top: shows mast base at 90° to the mast centre line, therefore compression X is in line with centre line of base, and there is no bending moment because Y is zero. Middle: has a flat mast base, and the base is not at 90° to the mast. Here there is a large distance Y which creates a large bending moment. Bottom: is as B, but the mast has a curved base, so the contact point is closer to the mast centre line, therefore distance Y is reduced, and so is the bending moment.

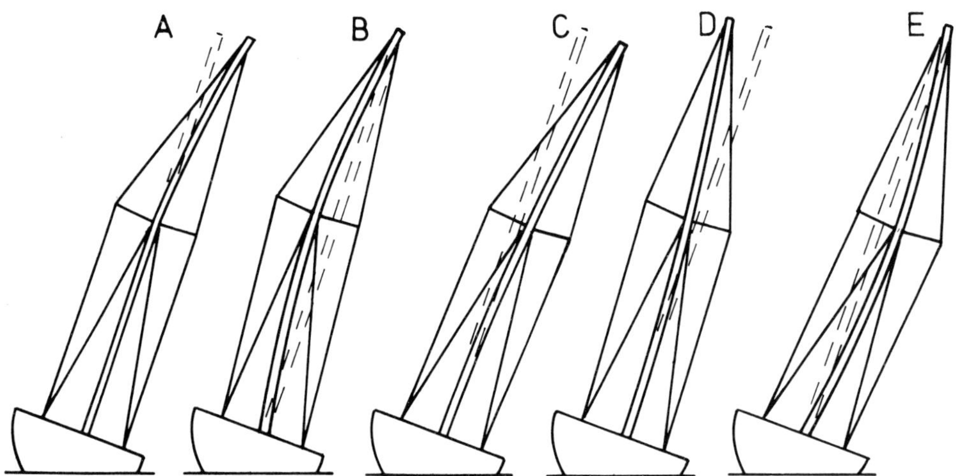

9. Stay adjustments. A: cap shrouds too slack. B: lowers too tight. C: caps and lowers too slack. D: caps and lowers too tight. E: lowers too slack.

brought on by fatigue; besides which it is awkward (and expensive) for the amateur to handle.

It is important to be able to tell how much you are stretching various shrouds and stays. Good instruments for measuring the tension in wire are expensive, and it is therefore not practical for each individual boat owner to have his own. One easy method of obtaining an approximate figure of the loadings in any wire is to measure the stretch. Within half the breaking strength, the stretch of stainless steel wire is almost linear to the load, and the following empirical formula can be used.

$$\text{load(kg)} = \frac{\text{elongation(cm)} \times \text{breaking load(kg)}}{\text{stretched wire length(m)}}$$

Therefore, a 10 metre wire is stretched 5cm when the load is increased from zero to half the breaking strength. So to use this information in estimating or calculating the load in the wire, it will be necessary to take the slackness out of it, but be careful not to put any real load on. Mark on this wire a dimension of 1980mm as accurately as possible; use tape or a marking pen for this purpose. With the use of the above formula, you will see that for every millimetre the measured length of 1980mm increases, the load in the wire has increased by five per cent of the breaking strength of the wire. Therefore when your dimension reaches 1985mm this should be considered the critical point, as the wire now has twenty-five per cent of the breaking load of the wire on it. This is critical from the point of view of stretch, rather than risk of failure. Risk of failure will only occur at around fifty per cent of the breaking load of the wire. The mast will be difficult to tune with such high stretch in the wires and, if you find yourself dealing with such loads, consider fitting larger diameter wire, thus making tuning easier, and the rig safer.

Table 2. List of Breaking Loads of 1 × 19 SS Wire

Wire diameter	Breaking load (kgs)	Newtons
3mm	(720)	7063
4mm	(1280)	12556
5mm	(2000)	19620
6mm	(2880)	28252
7mm	(3550)	34825
8mm	(4640)	45518

Earlier in this chapter, a load of ten per cent of the yacht's displacement was given for the static load of the cap shrouds. This figure was given on the normal understanding that

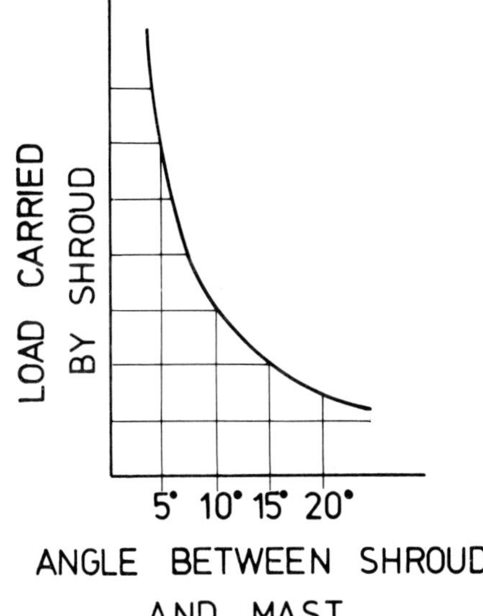

10. Graph shows the reducing load in the shrouds with the increase in the angle between shroud and mast. This increase is usually achieved by lengthening the spreaders.

the angle of the upper shrouds to the mast was between ten and eleven degrees; this is 175mm to 195mm of spreader length for every metre of vertical distance between the upper shroud fastening on the mast and the spreader (see fig. 7). It is usually not advisable to go below this angle, as extra tension would have to be put on the cap shroud, which would in turn give extra compression in the mast and additional stretch in the wire, possibly necessitating use of a larger diameter cap shroud to keep the mast straight athwartships (fig. 10).

In order to keep the mast straight when sailing to windward in heavy weather, it may be necessary to give extra tension to the backstay, because the top of the mast will tend to bend forward and to leeward above the spreaders. If the yacht is fitted with a wheel adjuster or hydraulics, this adjustment is easily made. So, when tuning the mast, it is advisable for the mast top to be slightly aft and to windward of a straight line in light weather. Should the mast tend to curve into an S, the extrusion profile could be too weak, in which case you should contact your mast maker immediately. Another sign of a weak mast is if the section between the spreaders and the mast top is straight, but the mast is bent below the spreaders. The most common indications that the mast is correct but that the rigging is not suitable, are that the mast is straight from the step to the spreaders but thereafter bent, or, even though the mast top is bent slightly to windward in light airs as mentioned previously, it bends excessively to leeward in heavy winds. If, after checking that the wire diameter is correct and that you are working within the correct loadings in the wire, the mast top is still proving uncontrollable, it is possible that the mast step or chain plates are moving. This may be an indication of poorly fastened chainplates, inadequately reinforced mast step or a soft hull.

Chocking Keel-Stepped Masts at the Partners

The following mast chocking system is recommended because it is desirable that the mast is held very firmly at deck level to secure maximum effective strength from the spar, and it is helpful if the mast is free to move sideways a small amount, to compensate for the inevitable stretch of the shrouds.

1. Any form of hard rubber may be used for the mast chocks: this is obtainable in most thicknesses of material, and can be cut from sheet. The type of rubber used should be compressible to a small extent, but not soft and spongy. The dimensions given for the thicknesses of rubber to be used depend on the amount these rubber strips are compressible. For the purpose of this article, it is assumed that a rubber strip is used that will compress twenty-five to thirty per cent of its thickness.

2. The deck partner faces should be vertical and parallel to the face of the mast, and should not be bevelled, rounded or angled.

3. The chock should be cut from the appropriate thickness of material and made to the correct width and height with parallel faces (as per fig. 11).

4. Only two chocks should be used, which should be cut to the proper shape and size as fig. 11. There should be one on the forward and one on the aft side of the mast.

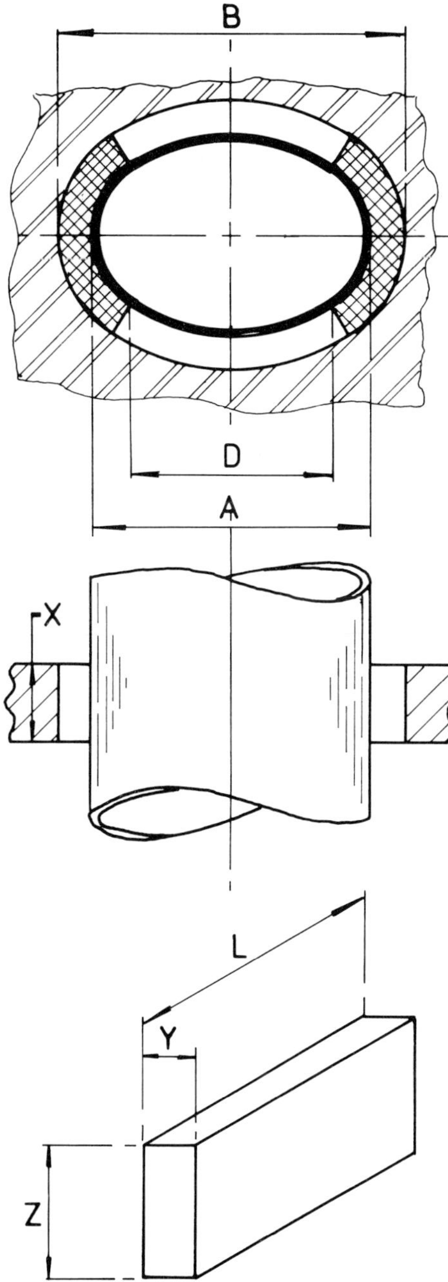

5. The height of the chocks should be 12-15mm above the top of the rigid partners and the bottom should extend 50mm or so below the partners. This gives enough length at the bottom to attach a jubilee clip or hose clamp, to prevent the wedges falling out when the mast is working in a seaway (fig. 12).

6. The two chocks should be equal in thickness so that the mast is centred in the partners. The total thickness of the chocks should be approximately one hundred and twenty-five per cent of the gap available, although this will depend on the type of material used for chocking. A more flexible material would have to be up to one hundred and fifty per cent of the gap available, whereas a more rigid material would probably only have to be one hundred and five per cent to one hundred and ten per cent of the gap width (fig. 11).

7. It is better to insert the chocks from below deck, as this permits the semi-permanent installation of the mast coat and clips to be left in position while any later adjustment to the chocks is carried out from

11. Mast chocking. Top: plan view of deck aperture showing the mast and rubber chocks. B: fore and aft dimension of deck partners. A: mast fore and aft dimension. D: 30 per cent of C. C: mast circumference. Middle: the fore and aft view of the mast and section through the deck partners (X is width of deck partners). Bottom: the rubber chock where L is 30 per cent of C. $Z = X + 65mm$*, and* $Y = \frac{(A-B)}{2} \times 1{\cdot}25$.

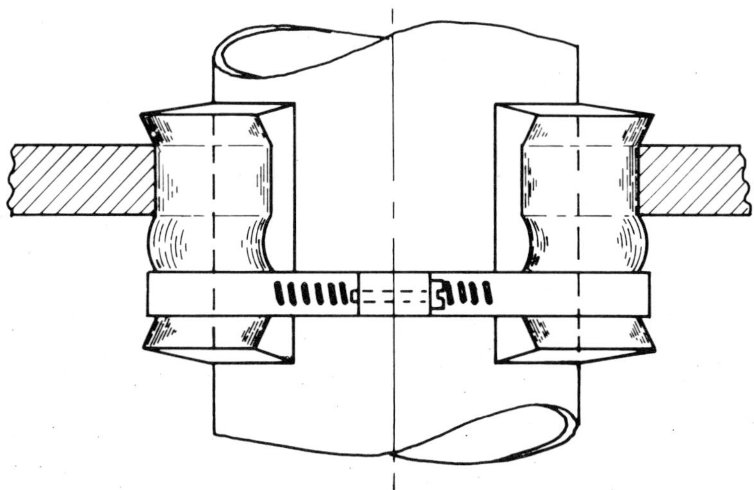

12. The fore and aft deck partners sectioned showing the rubber chocks compressed and held in position by a jubilee clip or hose clamp. Note the 12-15mm projection above the partners.

inside the boat. This allows the water tight seal (which is so difficult to achieve) to be left undisturbed during the rig tuning operation.

8. *Installation* Leave all the rigging slack. Rig a multi-part handy billy with a rope strop around the mast just above deck level (fig. 13). Fit the first chock in place; this should be the one that is the most difficult to get at, perhaps because of the proximity to any bulkhead etc. Make up on the handy billy with enough power to compress the chock that is already in place, so as to provide room for the second chock to be slid in. Then release the handy billy, and this will leave the mast centred in the partners with both rubber chocks under compression. It is advisable to use a jubilee clip to hold the rubber in position. This will prevent the rubber being shaken loose under sailing conditions, and will also make tidier the flared appearance of the rubber chocks below deck.

9. The most effective material for the mast coat is neoprene rubber. The rubber can be covered with dacron or canvas to protect it from the sun or accidental damage, and this gives a more attractive appearance (plate 6).

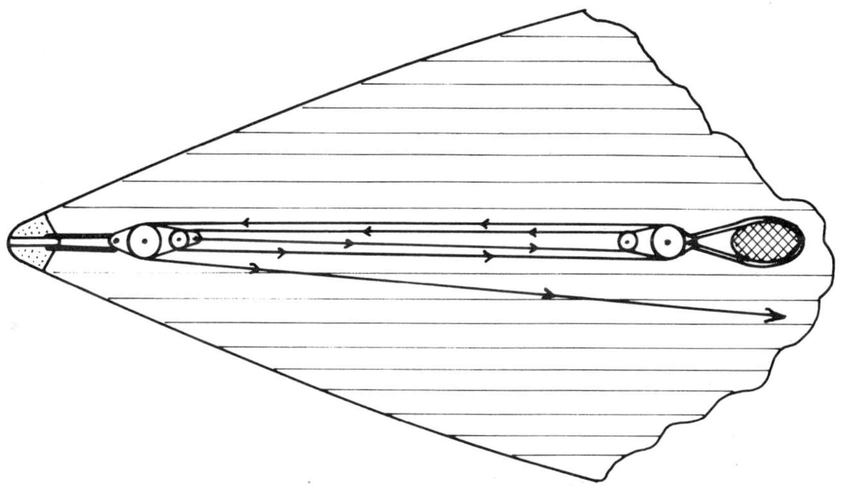

13. The mast should be pulled forward with the block and tackle for the insertion of the aft chock. The forward chock is inserted before the tackle is tightened.

Plate 6. Sealing masts at deck level. A cut-away view of a mast at deck level, showing the deck ring that would be fitted to the yacht, the rubber chocking between the deck ring or mast partners, and the mast and the rubber mast coat and clips that prevent water running down the outside of the mast and entering the yacht between the ring and mast. The large white area on the inside of the mast is an internal seal that stops water running down. Note the drain hole in the back of the mast close above the deck seal.

four

Standing and Running Rigging

The type of wire best suited to any application depends on the amount of stretch which can be tolerated and the degree of flexibility required.

Stretch

The fewer the strands in a wire rope, the less stretch and flexibility there will be, and the higher the breaking load. Figure 14 shows how a wire of 1 × 19 construction has a higher breaking load and less stretch than one of 7 × 19.

A racing yacht needs a forestay in particular where stretch is reduced to the minimum, in an attempt to eliminate sag; main shrouds are also candidates. To this end, wire of single strand construction would appear to be the obvious solution, in other words: solid rod. But we have seen that reduction in stretch has to be paid for by poorer flexibility. This means that rod should only be used for standing rigging, and even here it should be regarded with suspicion because of the danger of failure through fatigue.

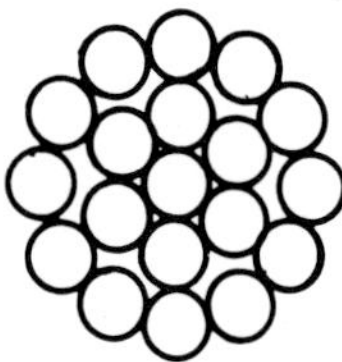

14. Top: 1 × 19 wire rope is nineteen single strands. Bottom: 7 × 19 wire rope is seven strands each containing nineteen wires.

Flexibility

On any standing rigging there are side forces trying to pull the rods out of a straight tension line; this is particularly true of the forestay. Every time the boat tacks, the genoa works on

Table 3. Comparisons between breaking loads of 1 × 19 and 7 × 19 ss wire

Wire diameter	1 × 19 breaking load		7 × 19 breaking load	
	(kgs)	Newtons	(kgs)	Newtons
2·5mm	(500)	4905	(370)	3630
3·0mm	(720)	7063	(464)	4552
4·0mm	(1280)	12556	(729)	7151
5·0mm	(2000)	19620	(1225)	12017
6·0mm	(2880)	28252	(1867)	18315
7·0mm	(3550)	34825	(2508)	24603
8·0mm	(4640)	45518	(3018)	29606

Table 3. Wire Breaking Loads (2).

the forestay; as the mast is bent, the shrouds are deflected by the spreaders; the backstay can be pulled out of line by crew members using it as a handhold when looking over the stern. All these small deflections build up a fatigue cycle which is aggravated by tension loadings and which will ultimately end in the rods breaking. I would estimate the safe working life of rod rigging under normal conditions to be no better than two seasons. So the benefits of low stretch have to be considered against poor life expectancy. If low stretch is all-important to you, and you are prepared to grapple with the problems of dressing a mast with something which will not bend other than in a large circle, spend the extra money, but be prepared to renew it all after a couple of years, even though it shows no external sign of fatigue. While you are about it (and assuming that you have a racing boat–otherwise why go to the expense of rod rigging?), you could equally well invest in a solid head-foil, for groove luff jibs. This suffers from the same awkwardness in handling as rod rigging and even greater expense. If you decide to take my advice and adopt 1×19 wire for your standing rigging, you can still have a head-foil by using one of the many alloy or even plastic extrusions which can be fed over the forestay wire.

If full flexibility is required, as in the case of running rigging which has to bend over sheaves, even 1×19 wire is not sufficiently tolerant; you will have to go to 7×19 construction, because the larger number of smaller strands used in a given size wire are necessary where constant bending round a fairly small radius will take place. The most universally-used wires are 1×19 construction for standing rigging and 7×19 construction for running rigging.

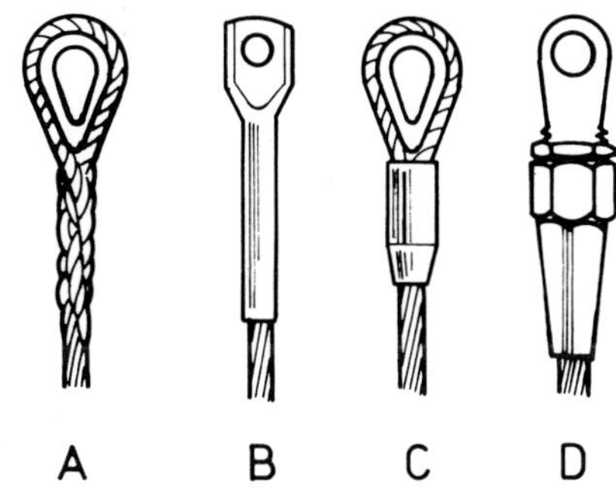

15. A: Hand eye splice. B: Rolled swaged eye terminal. C: Talurit eye splice; Nicopress is similar. D: Norseman (bolt-on) eye terminal; Sta-lock and Electroline are similar.

Standing Rigging Terminations

There are four principal methods of terminating standing rigging wire, as shown in fig. 15. These are firstly, the hand splice, and secondly, the Talurit or Nicopress terminal, which is the process of forming the wire around a thimble, and clenching the wires together with a copper ferrule (see plates 7 and 8). The third method is the roll swaged terminal:

Plate 7. A Talurit press in operation. The two halves of the press come together (the gap between the two parts of the press can be seen by the centre of the eye), squeezing the copper ferrule round the wire. Operation of a Nicopress is similar.

Plate 8. Talurit eye. A Talurit eye that has just come out of the press. Note the raised web on the top and bottom of the ferrule, caused when the two halves of the press come together. This is the surplus material which is filed off. Also note the projection of the tail of the wire through the right hand side of the ferrule: the wire should project 50 per cent of the wire diameter. The wire shown is 6mm (1/4in) diameter, and even on this size of wire (1 × 19) you can see the separation of the strands as they bend tightly round the thimble. The larger the wire, the worse this separation; 7mm (5/16in) diameter is recommended as the maximum size for this type of splice.

this is a stainless steel fitting which is passed over the wire, and the shank of this fitting is then rolled down, gripping the wire tightly (see plate 9). The fourth method is the bolt-on type, known as the 'Sta-lock', 'Electroline' or 'Norseman' terminal. This termination is the only hand, as opposed to machine, method of terminating the wire. All three methods are widely in use today and internationally accepted. The Talurit is the cheapest, but is only recommended on diameters of up to 6mm or 7mm; above this size the wire becomes deformed with the lays separated through bending round the tight radius of the thimble. The swaged termination is perhaps the neatest and most professional-looking of all four, but probably the most expensive because of the specialised equipment needed to form these terminals on to the wire. The bolt-on terminal is ideal for the do-it-yourself expert, as very few tools are needed (see fig. 16). Their other advantage is that spares can be carried on board, so if at any time you are stranded away from professional riggers, you can make your own repairs. Each of these terminals comes in its

Plate 9. A roll swage press in operation. The two cut-away circular wheels rotate (the top one clockwise and the lower one anti-clockwise), compressing the shank of the terminal and forcing the material to form round the wire.

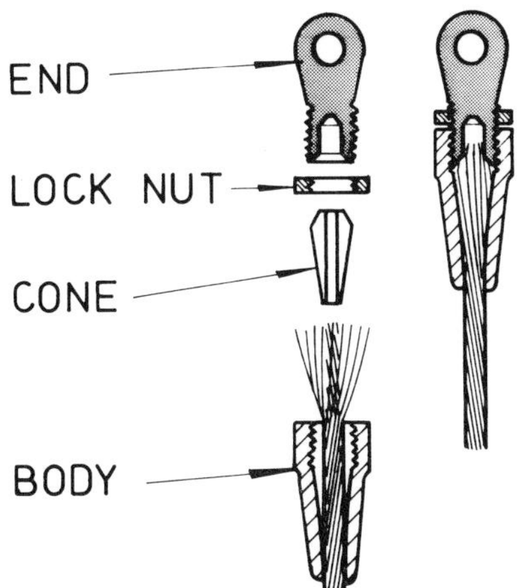

16. Norseman eye terminal: component parts and assembled.

own plastic sealed packet with full instructions. However, two points need special attention.

First, ensure that silicone rubber is squeezed into the terminal end; this prevents water running down the lays of strands and seating there, thus accelerating corrosion. Second, ensure that a thread locking sealant is put on all the threads, to prevent the body and lock nut becoming loosened from the the terminal end.

Norseman Terminal Fitting Instructions (see fig. 17)

1. Use good pre-formed wire rope only; cut clean end with sharp cutters.
2. Select correct cones for size of 1 × 19 wire.
3. Pass rope through body and prise away outer strand of wire.
4. Press cone down over central strand of wire to a depth equal to the wire diameter.
5. Bend outer wires of strands over cone.

6. and 7. Screw end units into body and tighten.

8. Unscrew assembly to make sure wires are evenly spaced and have completely closed over cone.
9. Re-assemble, filling with silicone rubber sealant, and preferably using a thread locking sealant; tighten lock nut.
10. Heat shrink sleeve, if used with plastic protected wire ropes. If this type of termi-

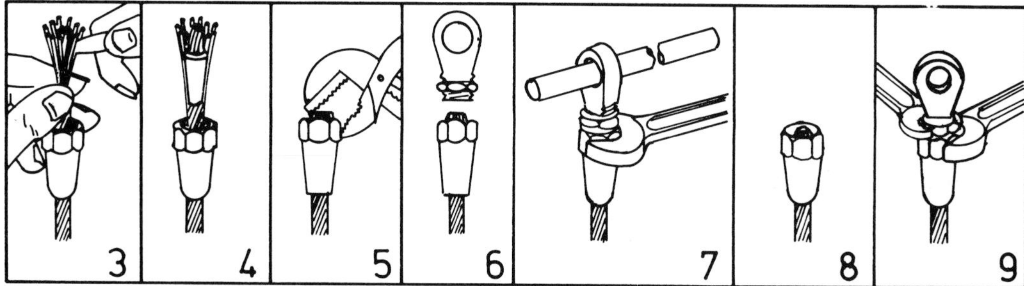

17. Fitting instructions diagram for Norseman terminals.

nation ever has to be removed from the wire, it is essential that a new cone is fitted when replacing the terminal.

Annual Maintenance and Inspection

The wires should be washed to rid them of all salt and dirt, dried and stored for the winter. The areas where failure will first occur will be around terminations. To inspect for potential damage, bend the wire gently where the termination finishes and look for any loose strands or spikes or wire that may appear. The same procedure should be adopted throughout the length of the wire as any loose spikes or strands that may be sticking through the outer strands of the wire, or indeed any stranding or fraying of the outer wires themselves, are the first signs of trouble. These wires should be replaced immediately, or at the very least you should consult your local rigging expert (see plates 10 and 11).

Running Rigging

When using 7×19 wire for halyards, it is normal to use only Talurit or Nicopress terminations. The wire lends itself perfectly to this method, because it has greater flexibility and does not suffer when bent round the stainless steel thimble. To locate faults, adopt the same inspection procedure as for standing rigging. If these halyards are spliced to rope tails, look for loose strands of wire sticking through the area of the wire-to-rope splice, also look for signs of strain on the rope in the spliced area (see plate 12). Reductions in the rope diameter in the area of a splice are often one of the first signs that the wire-to-rope splice is being strained. When storing halyards for the winter, it is important to wash them out in fresh water, as salt particles are easily trapped in the rope tails. If galvanised running rigging is used, a light coating of linseed oil will be of benefit after the wire has been washed and throughly dried. Be sure to label all wires carefully, then coil and put away for the winter.

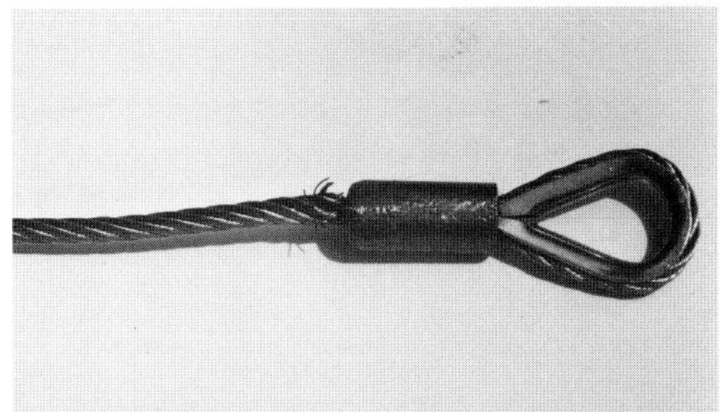

Plate 11. Talurit eye failure. The first signs of fatigue in a pressed wire rope splice will be the strands of the wire projecting through the outer layers of the wire. The photograph shows these wires projecting just behind the Talurit ferrule. It may be necessary to bend the wire gently at this point to see the first of the broken strands. When a wire reaches this stage of fatigue, many of the internal wires will be broken, thus reducing its strength. Such splices should be replaced at the first signs of the breakdown.

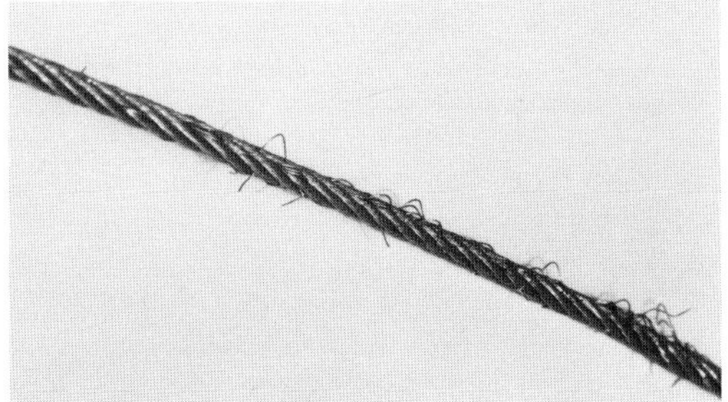

Plate 10. Wire failure. A wire that is fatigued and over-stressed will have spikes of wire projecting through the outer surface–so-called gashers or whiskers. The photograph shows an advanced stage of the breakdown. This wire should have been replaced long before so many whiskers appeared.

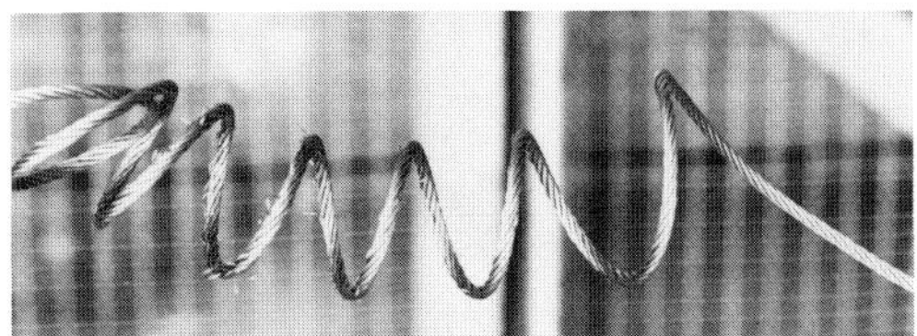

Plate 12. A wire that has been dragged round a static fairing, or a sheave with too small a radius, will suffer permanent deformation. The photograph shows a wire that has been running round a steel fairing. When this halyard is slackened off, it forms a tight spiral of spring-like appearance. When a wire takes this natural set, it is already fatigued and will soon fail. The minimum diameter of any sheave should be at least twelve times the diameter of the wire in question.

five
The Masthead Rig

This chapter is intended to deal with all the principal fittings on the single- and double-spreader masthead rig, giving indications of the type of forces and problems that can be expected in each fitting, together with points on maintenance.

Masthead Fitting or Head Box

Basically there are two types of head box in use today. One is welded in and the other is bolted on. Both are made from extrusions rather than cast. Cast headboxes are always a little suspect, as quality cannot be guaranteed, and cast flaws can occur at points of high stress, resulting in inevitable failure.

Casting relies on molten metal being poured into a form which may be of fired sand or steel. A good casting relies on many areas of human control, which as we all know can be subject to the mood and temperament of the operator. The molten metal has to be of correct temperature and fluidity at time of pouring. The mould also has to be at the correct temperature. If either or both of these points are not met, the material will chill and solidfy before it fills the contours of the mould. As the molten metal cools, it contracts, and will try to draw metal away from other parts of the die, leaving areas wasted, or hollow. To overcome this, risers (columns of molten alloy), are fed into the mould at various points so that the contracting casting can draw metal from these reservoirs. The

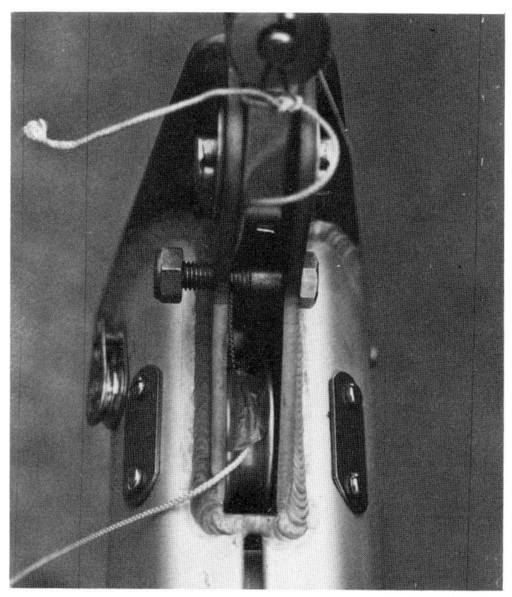

Plate 13. To remove a sheave from a masthead fitting that is welded in, follow the sequence of the five photographs so that you do not lose the sheave or bush down the inside of the mast. (a) *Tape a thin messenger line about 300 or 400mm long (just over one foot) to the sheave.* (b) *Rotate the sheave until the taped end of the messenger appears.* (c) *Remove the tape and the end of the messenger so that the line forms a complete loop around the sheave.* (d) *Keeping light tension on the loop round the sheave, remove the cover plates and sheave axle.* (e) *Lift sheave and bush out of head box housing. Re-assemble in reverse way.*

positioning of these risers is usually in the hands of the foundry. Aluminium alloys undergo changes in their chemical and molecular structures during cooling. These changes, if not correctly controlled, can cause coarse grains and brittleness. It is only the addition of certain chemicals in correct proportions, when the melt is poured into the mould, that prevents this change. All these processes are in the hands of the foundry and

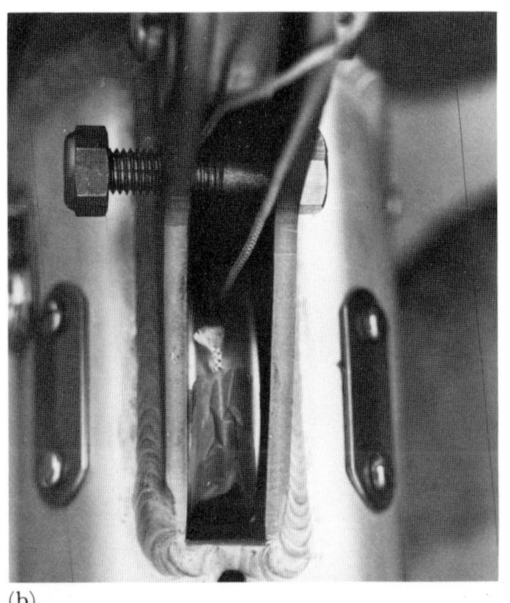
(b)

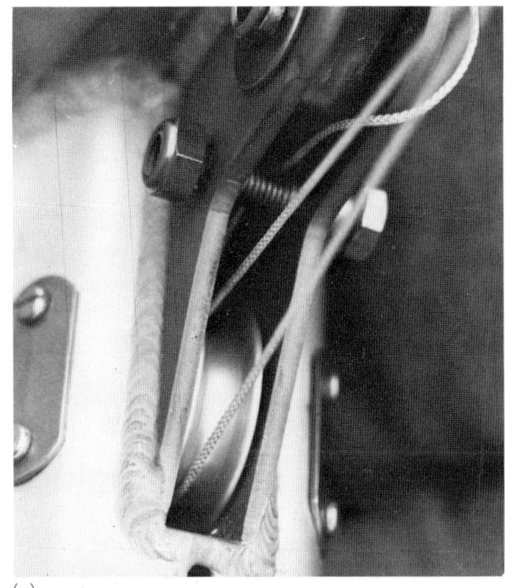
(c)

(d)

(e)

skill of the foundry operator. Few of the above errors can be detected by visual inspection; porosity in the casting or brittleness in the alloy will only be seen after dissection, and in the second case, only under a microscope. Castings are excellent for use in less structural areas, but in view of the problems of quality control, they cannot have much to recommend them for use in areas of high stress, where lives can depend on their reliability and consistency.

The welded-in type of head box becomes an intrinsic part of the mast structure and can never be removed, or have any of its main structural parts replaced, without major surgery by the spar maker. Only the sheaves and toggles may be replaced, and this is sometimes a very difficult operation: through-pins have to be removed for the sheaves to be withdrawn. The danger is that, as the through-pin is removed, the sheave can fall to the inside of the mast. One way of preventing this is to run a thin nylon messenger line around the sheave so that, as the pin is removed, the messenger will lift it out of the housing (see plate 13). The disadvantage with this type of head box is that when you wish to re-run halyards, you are unable to see down inside the mast to observe what is happening to the halyard messengers. This also applies to the problem of halyards jamming inside the mast: it would be impossible to see the area of trouble and you would be working in the dark. A removable head box allows clear vision down inside the mast for repairs or maintenance to take place including the re-running of halyards. Also, having the complete unit removable means that any maintenance or repairs on the head box can be carried out in the comfort of the workshop, and none of the box can be lost down inside the mast (plate 14). The head box needs very little location to hold it in the mast section, although spar makers using this type of head fitting use very strong and secure fastenings for this purpose. The welded-in boxes need no location of course, but the only problem that has been observed is the localised annealing, caused by the heat generated by the welding operation of fitting the boxes in the mast section. This has

Plate 14. Bolted-in headbox, showing the U bolt on the forward starboard side of the box which will take the spinnaker halyard. Also, you can just see the two holes for the port side U bolt, should a second halyard be required.

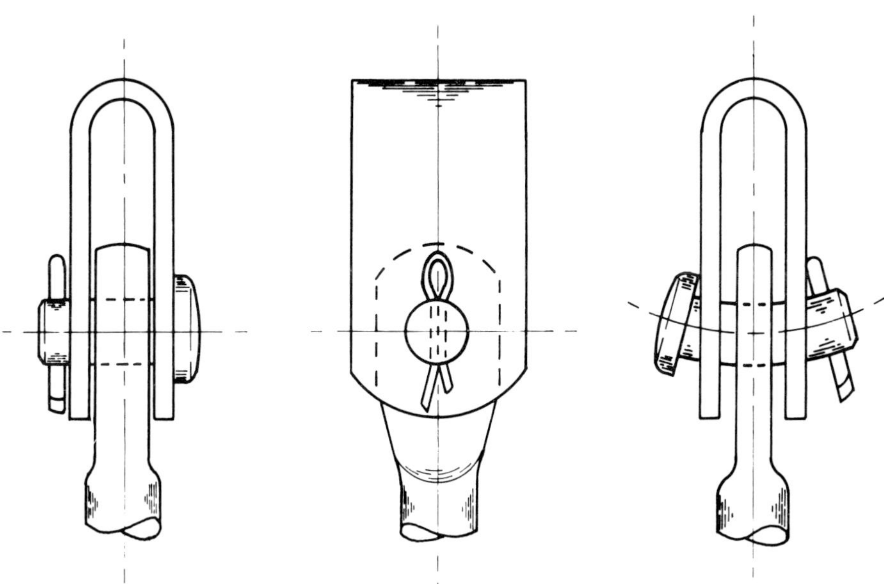

18. Left: swaged eye terminal correctly fitted in strip toggle; note clearance between eye and toggle is only about 10 per cent of gap width. Free movement of clevis pin is only 0-5 per cent of gap width, so toggle cannot open or spread. Middle: same eye and toggle split pin opened to 30°. Right: similar toggle and eye terminal, but here the clearance between eye and toggle, and the use of a clevis pin that is too long for the application, have been the causes of the bending of the clevis pin, which will soon shear.

caused mast failures due to the softening of the alloy near to the attachment points of the forestay and backstay toggles. It is, however, fair to say that in the majority of cases, the trouble has been caused by welders who are not experienced in the problems and stresses encountered in yacht mast design. Most spar manufacturers today have this problem well and truly covered, and there should be no fear of failure in this area.

Maintenance

Like all marine fittings that have moving parts, the head box is subject to salt water crystallisation, and lack of lubrication will cause severe wear on the bearings, sheaves and pins. The type of maintenance required very much depends on the type of materials used in the head box, but in all cases they should be kept clear of salt particles. In those head boxes where the bearings are made of nylon-reinforced composite material, which is water-lubricated, little oiling, if any, should be necessary. Because of the high loads imposed on the sheaves, it is not normally sufficient to make the bearing materials out of nylon. These materials have to be reinforced with carbon or glass fibres; PTFE is often used in these composites to give better frictional properties. However, no matter which material the bushes are made from in your head box, treatment with an aerosol lubricant or a light penetrating and lubricating oil will not do any harm after the salt crystals have been throughly washed away. Other areas requiring inspection in the head box are the forestay and backstay toggles, and the bearing pins for the toggles in the head box. When examining these, look for elongation of the holes through which the pins pass, and ensure that the pins are not being bent because the eye of the rigging terminal is too slack in the toggle (see fig. 18). Always ensure that split pins retaining any part of the head box, toggle or rigging are opened to a minimum of 30°. On head boxes where spinnaker halyards are in a vulnerable position, make sure that the split pins are well taped to prevent snagging on the spinnaker.

A lot of sheave bushes are made from tufnol. These bushes, when left to run dry, wear very badly, and eventually the hole becomes so large that the sheave stops turning. Inspect the head box regularly and, with the weight off the halyards, ensure that there is not excessive vertical play in the sheaves. Also, if your halyards are tight and not free running, do not continue to hoist the sails hoping that things will improve, go aloft and look at the sheaves. If these have stopped turning, not only will the bushes have to be replaced, but possibly the sheaves and your halyards. Once the sheaves stop turning, the halyards, with continual winching, will score a groove in the sheave, and the halyard being dragged over this static point will be subject to fatigue and possible failure.

Plate 15. A spinnaker halyard led over a swivel block will always have the fall of the halyard in the same plane, so that leading the halyard internally is very simple. The photograph shows a fairing on the front quarter of the mast which guides the halyard inside it.

Spinnaker Halyard

The spinnaker halyard generally runs through

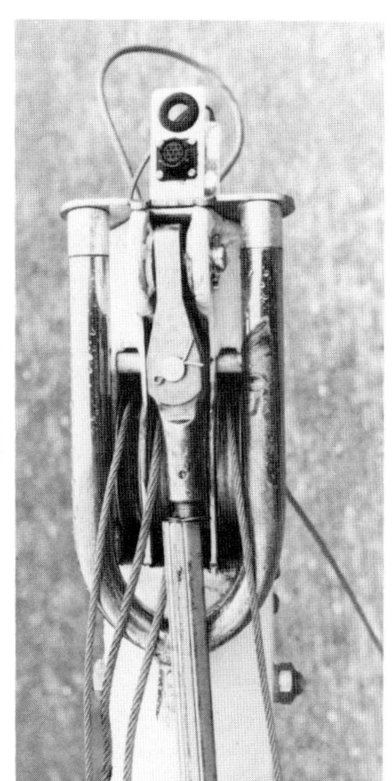

Plate 16. Spinnaker led internally round fairings. Three types of masthead fittings where the spinnaker halyard runs round a fairing. Note the chafe that has taken place due to the activity of the spinnaker halyard. It is probable that these halyards are changed two or three times a season.

a block hung on a U bolt on the head box. The fall of the halyard may be taken either internally about one metre from the mast head or may be run externally down the mast throughout its complete length (plate 15). This method is relatively trouble-free and is very fair on the halyard, as the block automatically turns to take up the correct alignment. The fall of the halyard is always in the same line, but the pull of the spinnaker will vary with the boat's angle to the wind. The halyard with this system is therefore always in a direct line and not subject to fatigue. The alternative is to have the halyard entering the mast via a fairing (see plate 16 and fig. 19). As can be seen, this type of spinnaker entry is neat and low on windage. The problem with it is that the halyard, when leaving the mast, is always running round the fairing to the port or starboard side. Any wire that runs

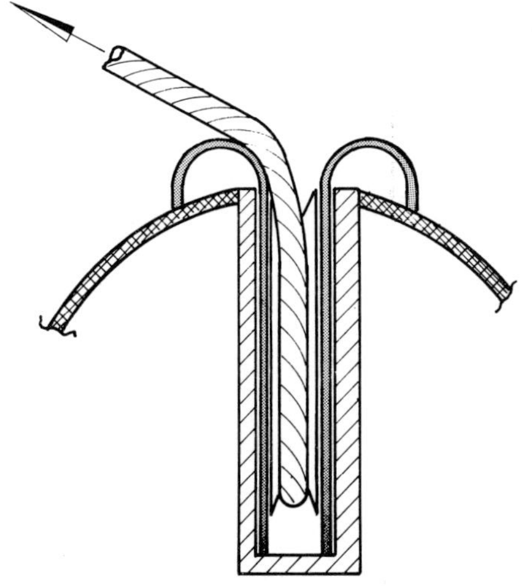

19. A wire or rope halyard that continually runs round a fairing will be subject to fatigue and failure, at the point where the halyard is constantly in contact with the fairing in the top 300mm (1ft) of a spinnaker halyard.

round such a fairing is subject to fatigue and will eventually break at this point. The other thing to consider with these two types of spinnaker entries is ease of use. The block fitted to the U bolt is low in friction and runs easily, thus making the hoisting and lowering of the spinnaker quick and trouble-free. With the halyard running round the fairing, additional friction occurs when hoisting the spinnaker on a reach, and in most cases it will be necessary to use a winch, thereby involving two crew members. Problems may also be found when lowering the spinnaker on a reach when the halyard is again tight up against the fairing, and high friction will be experienced, making lowering slow, and involving extra crew members who could be usefully employed elsewhere on the yacht at this time.

Shroud Attachments

There are two main methods of attaching shrouds to the mast: the T terminal and the fork tang (see plates 17 and 18). The advantage of the T terminal is that it makes dressing and undressing the mast a quick procedure. There are no split pins to open or close, and no sharp corners to catch on sails or halyards, causing wear and chafe. They are neat and streamlined in appearance and cause less windage aloft than any other form of attachment. T terminals are fitted to the shrouds in exactly the same way as the roll swaged eyes discussed in Chapter 4.

Maintenance and Fitting

This type of termination and attachment to the mast should require little or no maintenance, although inspection should not be neglected. Look for signs of stress in the T terminal where the right-angle bend occurs just before it enters the mast. If trouble should occur, small cracks may be seen starting from the inside of this radius. If this is observed, the

Plate 17. T terminal and spreader. Lower T terminal fitted into backing plate. Note wide base fastening of spreader socket, distributing the forces well round the mast.

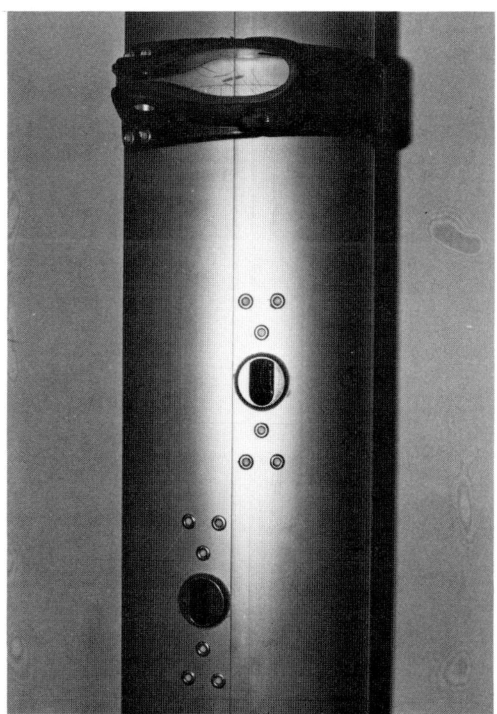

Plate 18. Double lower T terminal backing plates. Note the staggered heights of the holes and the spacing of the rivets, avoiding a peripheral line of holes or cut-outs.

terminals should be replaced immediately. The reinforced attachment plates which fit inside the mast should also be inspected regularly for any signs of distortion, or elongation of the slot. Look for any signs which may tell you that the rivets or screws that hold these plates in the mast are under strain, and see if any movement has occurred. Observe any local distortions in the mast wall, where bulging could occur due to the athwartships resultant force exerted by these terminals. If any of these problems become apparent, contact your mast maker immediately.

Maintenance and Inspection of Fork Tangs and Eye Terminals

Look for any signs of stress, strain or hole elongation in the eye terminal, and ensure that the eye terminal is a good close fit in the fork tang (see fig. 14). This also applies to the bending of the clevis pin and the opening of the split pin. Make sure that the mast through-bolts are locked by peening over the bolt or by split pinning the nut through the bolt. Any signs of these bolts slackening off should be rectified immediately by retightening and locking off. Make certain that the fastenings on any of the support plates under these bolts are in good condition and that there is no sign of any local stress or strain around the fastening of the plates. Look for any distortion in the mast wall local to any of these fittings.

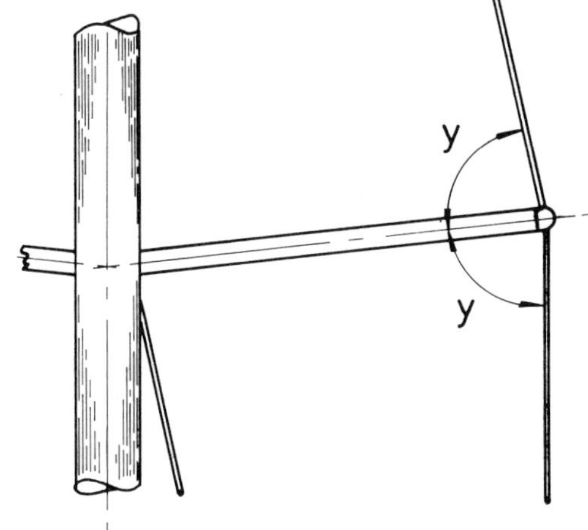

20. Angle y *should always be the same, the spreader must be firmly locked onto the cap shroud in this position.*

Spreaders and Sockets

The round tube spreader is designed only to withstand compression loads. This means that the mast must not be bent and that the spreader must always be bisecting the angle of the cap shroud (fig. 20). This type of spreader is best suited to the rigs which have fore and aft lowers, so that the mast is less likely to be deflected out of a straight line. If a clamp mechanism is available at the outer end of the spreader always ensure that this is securely tightened, and that the spreader is at the correct attitude at all times. All too often I observe masts in marinas with the spreaders horizontal or, worse, drooping below horizontal. When the compression load from the weather shroud is applied, a large bending moment is put on the spreader and unfair stresses imposed on the socket; this could either distort or bend the socket, or dent the mast wall beneath it. If there is not a clamp available at the end of the spreader for this purpose, then a bulldog grip (plate 19) can be locked onto the wire both above and below the spreader tip. Ensure that the outer end of the spreader is well padded and protected so that chafe on the genoa will be kept to a minimum. Spreader boots or anti-chafe

Plate 19. Bulldog grips or U-clamps make a useful addition to the spares kit for emergency repairs. At least two and preferably three clamps should be used for each eye. Care must be taken to ensure that all clamps are put on the same way, so that the shoulder or bridge grips the standing part and the U (or staple) grips the end. This is because the U tends to distort and weaken the wire, whereas the bridge does not; if the standing part is weakened, the whole line will suffer.

wheels are now obtainable from most yacht chandlers for this purpose. Many of the clamp-type fittings mentioned previously will have smooth and well-rounded ends which will serve as adequate protection for the genoa, and will need little other protection.

The streamlined spreader is subject to the same conditions as the round tube spreader, relating to the angle which bisects the cap shrouds. It is probably more important on

Plate 20. Spreader end clamp. Outboard end of spreader, showing the fitting clamped on to the cap shroud. Note the nut in the aperture which forces the two halves of the fitting together and clamps the wire. Also note the well-rounded face that will not harm a genoa.

streamlined spreaders than the round tube type, as they have a high section modulus fore and aft, but a low section modulus vertically. By this I mean that their resistance to fore and aft bend is great but their resistance to vertical bending is small because of the thin and streamlined profile. If they are allowed to come out of line, they will bend and fail easily. They are, however, a major structural feature of the mast, especially when the spar is being bent fore and aft to flatten the mainsail. As can be seen in fig. 21, when the mast is bent from the straight line, the tension in the shroud holds the outer tip of the spreader more or less in its original position, therefore the mast, moving forward at spreader height, will induce a bending moment on the spreader which, of course, it is well able to stand. This in turn produced structural problems on attachment to the mast, to such an extent that it is often necessary to strap the spreader sockets right round the front of the mast to get support from the opposite side. Through-bolting on the centre line is of little use in this instance, as the bolt is fastened on the pivot point. The danger is that the fastenings on the forward side of the mast will take all the strain and

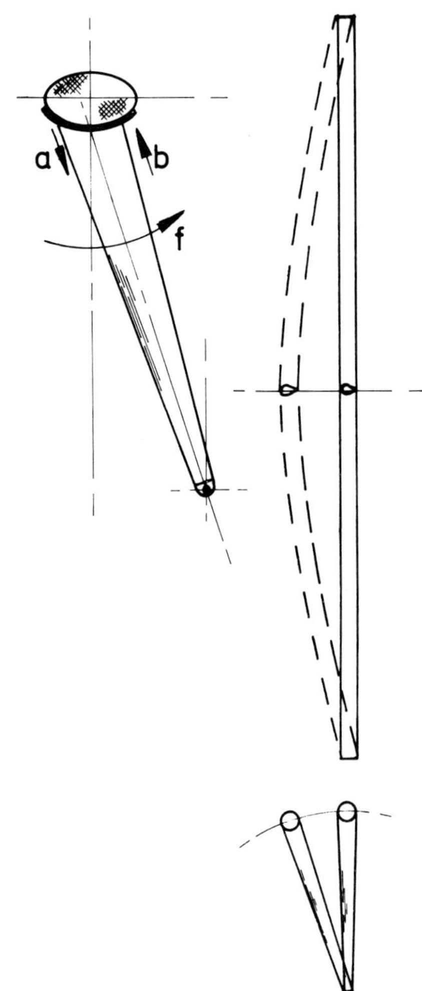

21. Right: mast bend. Bottom: plan view of the spreader, showing position before and after mast bend. Left: an enlarged view; f *is the torsional load caused by mast bend;* a *is the force which is acting away from the mast. Here the fastening must be very strong;* b *is a compressive force which will dent the mast if it is not distributed correctly to the mast wall.*

may not be strong enough; the fastenings on the aft side of the bracket are of little structural significance.

The other problem which can occur on the spreader bracket is that it may dent the mast. As you can see from fig. 21, there is a large force at the aft end of the spreader which will cause the mast wall to dent and collapse, if this load is not distributed correctly to the mast profile. If your spar maker advises you that all these structural conditions are met, the spreader will give increased stability to the centre of the mast when it is deflected from a straight line. This feature can result in the after lowers being brought much closer to the main chain plates than would otherwise be acceptable. I would emphasise again that if any owner is in any doubt about the structural suitability of his spreaders when bending the mast, he should contact his mast maker for further advice. One of the biggest growing causes of rig loss today is the failure of spreaders.

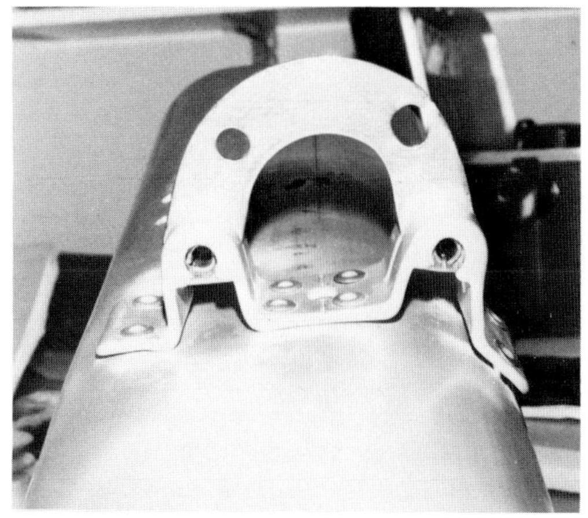

Plate 21. A failed spreader bracket. This bracket, like the round-tube-type spreader, was only designed to take compression. When tested for torsional resistance, it failed as shown. Note the dented mast by the aft foot of the bracket and strained rivets by forward foot (this bracket was symmetrical before testing). Also note the elongation and failure on the forward hole that attaches the spreader to the bracket.

Maintenance and Inspection

Maintenance should not be necessary as there are no moving parts, however, it is necessary to inspect several areas of the spreader and socket regularly. Starting at the outer end, ensure that the spreaders are securely fastened to the shrouds by any of the above methods and that the outer tips are protected against chafe on the genoa. Check all screws, nuts, bolts and split pins for wear and looseness, and correct as necessary. At the inboard end of streamlined spreaders, check that they are firmly held in their sockets. If there is any excessive fore and aft play, check for the cause of this looseness and consult your mast maker for further advice and remedial action. Check the socket fastenings to the mast, and look for any signs of stress or strain around these fastenings. Also look for any distortion that may have occurred on the mast wall, either at the front end, where it could bulge due to the bracket trying to pull away and the fastenings pulling at the section, and at the aft end for denting where the compression loads at the aft tip of the spreader have been distributed to the mast wall.

On tubular spreaders inspect the sockets; the socket is usually welded to the back plate and any weld is a suspect area, so check for cracks alongside the welds which join the socket to the backplate. As with streamlined spreaders, check all fastenings and look for any signs of distortion on the mast wall. Fore and aft play on a round tube spreader is acceptable. Most round tube spreaders are fitted into the sockets and have a rubber liner between the spreader and the socket. This is to allow a certain amount of play and relieve the above mentioned stresses and strains that only the streamlined spreaders can cope with. This rubber oı soft nylon liner will be subject to perishing, and should be checked and replaced every second or third season as necessary.

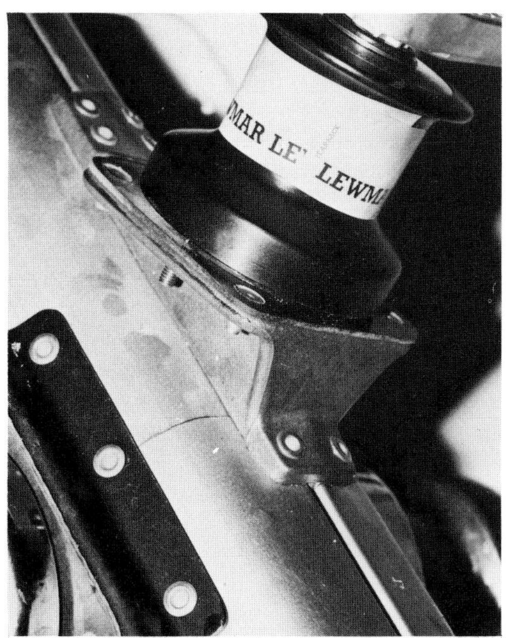

Plate 22. Insulator between mast and winch. Note the Tufnol (plastic) pad between the winch bracket and the winch. The insulator pad is riveted to the bracket in each corner (outside the winch base), and the bolt fastenings for the winch pass through the two. The thread on one of the fastenings can be seen on the left hand side of the angled winch.

Winch Brackets and Winches

These are mainly made of aluminium alloy, and pop riveted to the mast with monel or alloy rivets. The majority of winches have bronze bases which have a high electrolytic potential when put with aluminium alloy. It is therefore necessary and essential when fitting a winch to the mast that a suitable insulation material is used between the base and the winch pad (see plate 22); an inert material such as nylon or tufnol is recommended for this purpose. The winches are best fastened to the bracket with stainless steel machine screws. Stainless steel is better with bronze and aluminium than any other form of material, although it is not a perfect solution, and electrolytic action will occur over the years: I would recommend regular inspection. Using vaseline or mastic around the screw threads will give a small degree of protection.

Winches

The type of winch to be used for a particular application will depend very much on how hard the yacht will be sailed, and what degree of effort you are able to put into your sailing. The winch application chart (table 4) is therefore only intended as an approximate guide, assuming we are dealing with crews of average strength sailing monohull yachts of average displacement. Because I am most familiar with Lewmar winches, the reference numbers are those from their range, but other manufacturers will be able to give their own nearest equivalents quite easily if you prefer another product. The figures in brackets are area in square feet and length in feet, all other dimensions are in square metres and metres.

Lewmar No 6, 7, 8 and 10 winches are all single-speed.

Lewmar No 16, 30, 40 and 42 winches are all two-speed.

Lewmar No 44, 48, 55 and 65 winches are all three-speed.

Lewmar No 1H and 2H are single-speed, self-stowing (reel) winches.

Lewmar No 2.2H and 3H winches are double-speed, self-stowing (reel) winches.

Uses of Different Materials

Once you have decided which type and size of winches are right for your boat, you should consider whether chromed bronze or aluminium alloy construction are most suitable for your needs. Their advantages and availability are as follows:

Chromed Bronze: very rugged and suitable for all general purpose applications. Particularly recommended for cruising yachts and wire applications.

Aluminium Alloy: alloy with a black anodised finish was specially developed for racing boats because they are lighter. They are, however, only suitable for use with rope, because wire would cut into the surface.

Maintenance

Winches, like all other precision engineering products, must be serviced regularly as follows:

1. Every month all winches should be lightly oiled and greased with waterproof grease.

Table 4. Winch Application Chart

Length Overall metres (ft)		6·0 to 7·6 (20 to 25)	7·6 to 9·0 (25 to 29·5)	9·0 to 10·0 (29·5 to 33)	10·0 to 10·7 (33 to 35)	10·7 to 11·0 (35 to 36)	11·0 to 12·0 (36 to 39)	12·0 to 12·5 (39 to 41)	12·5 to 13·0 (41 to 43)	13·0 to 14·6 (43 to 48)
Approx Maximum Sail Areas. m² (sq ft)	Genoa	18 (200)	27 (300)	32 (350)	43 (470)	50 (550)	55 (600)	70 (750)	80 (900)	100 (1100)
	Spinnaker	27 (300)	37 (400)	55 (600)	75 (800)	95 (1000)	110 (1200)	130 (1400)	150 (1600)	175 (1900)
	Main	11 (120)	14 (150)	17 (180)	20 (210)	21 (230)	24 (260)	27 (300)	32 (350)	40 (420)
Genoa Sheet	Racing	No. 8	16 or 30	30 or 40	42 or 44	44 or 48	48 or 55	55	55 or 65	65
	Cruising	No. 7	10 or 16	30	40	42 or 44	44	44 or 48	48 or 55	55 or 65
Spinnaker Sheet	Racing	No. 6	No. 8	10 or 16	30 or 40	40 or 42	42	44	44 or 48	48 or 55
	Cruising	No. 6	No. 7	8 or 10	16 or 30	30	30 or 40	40	44	48
Main Sheet	Racing	Not Req.	Not Req.	8	16	30	30	40	40	42 or 55
	Cruising	Not Req.	Not Req.	6	7 or 10	10 or 16	16	30	30	40
Genoa Halyard	Racing	No. 8	16	30	30 or 40	40 or 42	44	44	44 or 48	48 or 55
	Cruising	No. 6	7	8 or 16	16 or 30	30	40 or 42	42	44	44
Spinnaker Halyard	Racing	No. 6	8	16	30	40	40 or 42	42	42	44 or 48
	Cruising	No. 6	7	7	8 or 10	16	16 or 30	30	40	42
Main Halyard	Racing	No. 6	6	8	10 or 16	30 or 40	40 or 1H	40 or 2H	40 or 2·2H	44 or 3H
	Cruising	No. 6	6	7	8 or 10	16 or 1H	16 or 1H	30 or 2H	30 or 2H	40 or 2·2H
Staysail Halyard	Racing	No. 8	8	16	30	30 or 40	40	40 or 42	42	44
	Cruising	No. 6	6 or 7	8	8 or 10	10 or 16	16	16 or 30	30 or 40	40
Spinnaker Pole T/Lift	Racing	Not Req.	Not Req.	Not Req.	7 or 8	8 or 10	10	10 or 16	16 or 30	30
	Cruising	Not Req.	Not Req.	Not Req.	6	8	8 or 10	10	16	16
Spin. Pole Foreguy	Racing	Not Req.	6	6	8	10 or 16	16	16 or 30	30	40
	Cruising	Not Req.	6	6	7	8 or 10	8 or 10	10	16	30
Leach Flat. & Clew Reef Lines	Racing	Not Req.	6	6	8	16	16 or 30	30	30 or 40	40 or 42
	Cruising	Not Req.	6	6	6	7	8	8	16 or 30	30

2. Two or three times during an active sailing season, all winches should be stripped, cleaned and re-lubricated, using the manufacturer's maintenance manual.

3. At the beginning and end of each season, all winches should be completely stripped, cleaned and lubricated, using the manufacturer's full maintenance manual.

General external cleaning of the drum: chromed winches should have the drum washed regularly with fresh water and dried with a chamois leather. Occasionally use non-abrasive liquid chrome cleaner to remove dirt deposits. Anodised alloy winches should have the drum washed regularly with fresh water and dried with a chamois leather. Do *not* use polishes or abrasives.

Cleats

The size of cleat for any given application is not usually judged by strength, but on its capacity to take the rope or line required. Any cleat should be able to accommodate three turns of rope or line; if this cannot be obtained, the cleat is undersize. It should, of course, not have hard corners which could cut or chafe.

Positioning on mast: the cleat should never be closer than 300mm (one foot) to the winch or exit box. It is sufficient to put the cleat on the mast vertically for most applications, but on masts where the cleat will be used in conjunction with a winch, it will be better to angle the cleat towards the centre of the winch drum so that it is 'open' to the lead. This means that, as the line comes off the drum, it will pass over the bottom of the cleat, any subsequent turns around the cleat will then clear the part of the halyard which is running from the cleat to the winch. If the cleat were to be fitted vertically, the part of the rope or line that goes to the winch would be running parallel to the cleat and resting hard against the other turns made round the cleat, thereby causing them to jam (see fig. 22).

Fastenings: It is best to fasten alloy cleats to the mast with either alloy or monel pop rivets. If riveting is not practical, it is acceptable to fit cleats with stainless steel self-tapping screws. If this method is used, ensure that correct length screws are used. Overlength screws will go right through the mast wall and may snag on internal halyards or wiring. Self-tapping screws made in stainless steel will have an electrolytic action between themselves and the alloy, and it is impossible to put an inhibitor on such fastenings as they have to be a tight fit in the hole. It is inevitable, over the years, that corrosion will occur, and any cleats fitted with stainless steel screws must be looked at on a regular basis for signs of loosening as the holding power of the screws is reduced through corrosion of the alloy.

Table 5 shows cleat size for size of yacht; the figures in brackets are in feet and in inches, the rest are in metres and millimetres.

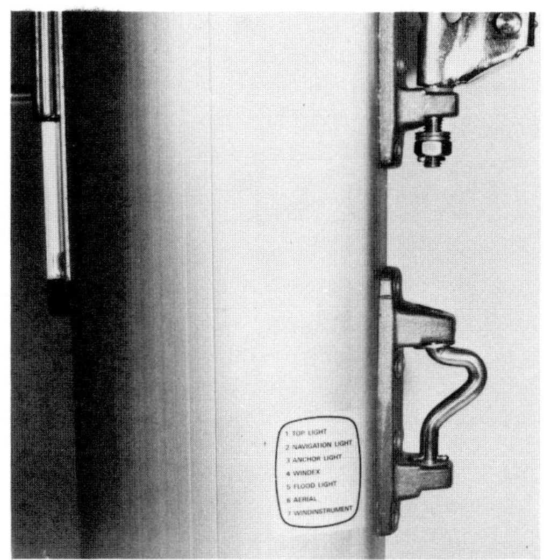

Plate 23. The kicking strap or boom vang and gooseneck are fitted close together on the demonstration mast, to show that the pivot for each unit is on the same vertical line.

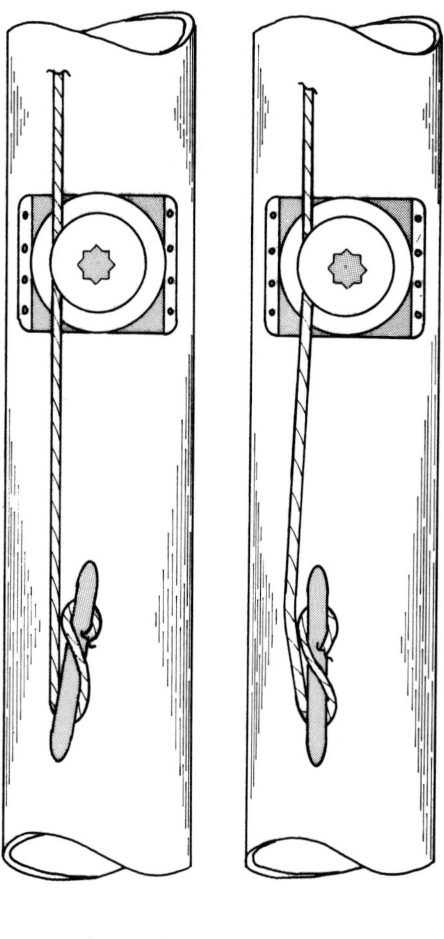

22. A: the cleat is angled so that the vertical part of the halyard is not jamming the line that is on the cleat. B: this cleat is fitted vertically so that the halyard is trapping the line that is on the cleat. The cleat fitted as in B could cause a delay in releasing the halyard.

Table 5. Cleat Sizes

Length Overall metres (ft) mm (in)	6·0 to 7·6 (20 to 25)	7·6 to 9·0 (25 to 29·5)	9·0 to 10·0 (29·5 to 33)	10·0 to 11·0 (33 to 36)	11·0 to 12·0 (36 to 39)	12·0 to 14·6 (39 to 48)
Burgee Halyard	100 (4″)	100 (4″)	100 (4″)	100 (4″)	100 (4″)	125 (5″)
Main Halyard	125 (5″)	125 (5″)	150 (6″)	200 (8″)	200 (8″)	250 (10″)
Genoa Halyard	125 (5″)	150 (6″)	200 (8″)	200 (8″)	250 (10″)	250 (10″)
Spinnaker Halyard	125 (5″)	125 (5″)	150 (6″)	200 (8″)	200 (8″)	250 (10″)
Spinnaker Boom Topping Lift	125 (5″)	125 (5″)	150 (6″)	150 (6″)	200 (8″)	200 (8″)
Main Boom Topping Lift	125 (5″)	125 (5″)	150 (6″)	150 (6″)	150 (6″)	200 (8″)

Kicking Strap or Boom Vang Fittings

Mast fittings for the vang or kicking strap generally take the form of a hoop bale or a fixed eye at the bottom of the mast. This is quite acceptable for block and tackle type kickers because, as I have mentioned before, stretch in the rope results in some give in the system which reduces the load on the fittings. This method of attachment to the mast must never be considered when using hydraulics, solid kicker vangs, or lever kicker assemblies, as these do not have much give. The attachments to the mast for these units must be fittings on vertical swivels. The vertical pin for such units should be on the same line as the vertical pivot pin of the main gooseneck. When the boom is squared off, the boom and kicking strap assembly then move in the same plane, so that there is no tightening or slackening effect on the kicker system with the movement of the main boom. To illustrate this point, plate 23 shows a main boom gooseneck fitted just a few centimetres from the kicking strap. By positioning the two fittings in this way, it can be seen clearly that the vertical pivot bolt of the gooseneck is in the same plane as the swivelling hoop of the kicking strap fitting.

six

Additions to a Masthead Rig

There are many extras which can be fitted to the standard rig. These can be done by the mast maker, but often they are added by an owner, once he has had time to evaluate any special requirements according to the type of sailing he intends doing. This chapter gives the more popular additions, with hints on how to fit them.

Electrical Wiring and Lights

On 15 July 1977 the International Regulations for Preventing Collisions at Sea (1972) came into force; annex I to the regulations contains data concerning the positioning and technical requirements of lights. All new yachts must comply with these regulations; even those which were built before July 1977, and benefited from a four year period of grace, must have changed their existing lights to conform by 1981.

There has been some change in thinking since the introduction of the new rules, so that the somewhat impractical red-over-green masthead combination is no longer popular. The principle of lights at the top of the mast is, however, sound, and the tri-colour red, green and white lantern which is permitted for yachts under 12 metres overall length when under sail, may be permitted in the future for use on those up to 20 metres

Plate 24. Navigation lights: for yachts up to 12 metres overall length, a tri-colour masthead lantern may be used when under sail.

Plate 25. Navigation lights: a 225° steaming light for yachts over 12 metres overall length.

overall (see plate 24). Apart from better visibility (the side lights are hoisted above the masking effect of headsails or the fact that the boat is heeled so that any light on the lee shroud is almost in the water; the stern light is well above the cabin top and possible shielding by liferaft, dodger or even upper-works), the advantage of this type of light is that power consumption is kept to a minimum, as only one bulb is required for all the lights which the vessel has to show when under sail; a second and important advantage is that the sectors covered by the lantern can be accurately determined by the manufacturer, so that there is no mounting of lights which overlap or show through incorrect angles providing it is correctly mounted fore and aft.

However, a yacht under power (and she is under power as soon as the auxiliary engine is turned on and propelling her, even though she may be sailing hard as well) must display a white light shining forward over an arc of 225°, which must be mounted at least one metre higher than the red and green side lights. This means that any sailing yacht which has an auxiliary motor and which has opted for the tri-colour lantern must also have side and stern lights mounted lower down, so that the white masthead light can be correctly shown above them when the engine is running.

There are further requirements regarding

Plate 26. Navigation lights: a combined deck and steaming light for yachts up to 12 metres overall length.

lights which, since they really only concern larger vessels, are not stringently interpreted for small boats even by the authorities. Strictly speaking, a small bilge keel trailer sailer, aground at night in two or three feet of water, should show two all-round red lights in a vertical line as well as her all-round white anchor light. She is plainly of no danger to anyone but herself, and the requirement is obviously ridiculous. Similarly a 30-foot yacht towing a Star or Dragon at night *should* show the special towing lights fore and aft but, providing she is ready to warn off any vessel attempting to cut through the narrow gap between her and her tow (by flashing code letter U: 'You are running into danger'), she need not be too concerned.

Annex I to the International Regulations also contains information on colour, intensity and visibility. The following is a brief summary of these requirements, but anyone proposing to fit his or her own lights should study the annex carefully.

Visibility

The annex gives a table for converting the luminous intensity of lights as expressed in candelas into visible range. Table 6 gives the minimum requirements.

In addition, the sectors through which the lights should be visible must be correct to within two degrees. There are some practical considerations contained in the regulations:

Table 6. Visibility Requirements for Navigation Lights

Light	**Under 20m overall**	**Under 12m overall**
Masthead	3 miles	2 miles
Side (red and green)	2 ,,	1 ,,
Stern	2 ,,	2 ,,
All-round (anchor etc)	2 ,,	2 ,,

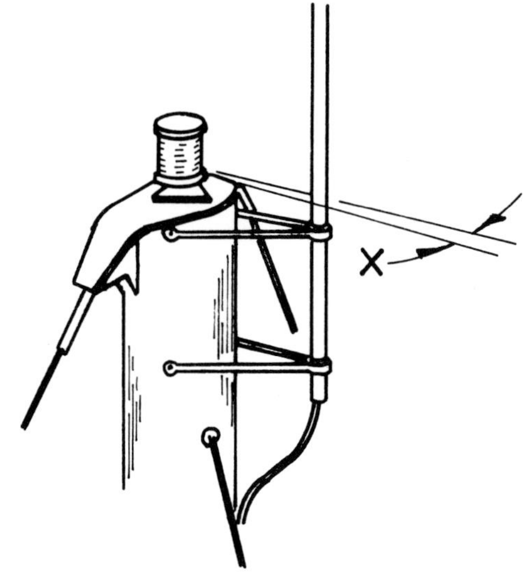

23. Navigation lights: no light shall be obscured by more than 6° of its arc.

Table 7. Electric Cable Sizes

		Length of cable															
Metres		2	4	6	8	10	12	14	16	18	20	25	30	35	40	45	50
Feet		7	13	20	26	33	39	46	52	59	66	82	99	115	131	148	164
Capacity required		**Wire diameter in square mm**															
Volts	**Watts**																
6	10	0·75	0·75	1·5	1·5	2·5	2·5	2·5	4·0	4·0	4·0	6·0	6·0	6·0	6·0		
6	25	1·5	2·5	4·0	4·0	6·0	6·0	6·0									
12	10	0·75	0·75	0·75	0·75	0·75	0·75	0·75	1·5	1·5	1·5	1·5	1·5	2·5	2·5	2·5	2·5
24	10	0·75	0·75	0·75	0·75	0·75	0·75	0·75	0·75	0·75	0·75	0·75	0·75	0·75	0·75	0·75	0·75
24	25	0·75	0·75	0·75	0·75	0·75	0·75	0·75	0·75	0·75	0·75	1·5	1·5	1·5	1·5	1·5	1·5
12	25	0·75	0·75	0·75	1·5	1·5	1·5	2·5	2·5	2·5	2·5	4·0	4·0	6·0	6·0	6·0	6·0

the lights must be water tight and it is not enough merely to fit lights with the correct nominal power, but without cables of the correct diameter for the job. The greater the run of wire from the power source, the greater the resistance and voltage drop, therefore a larger diameter wire has to be used. Ensure that the correct wires are used for your lights, bearing in mind the distance from the power source (see table 7).

When using a tri-colour masthead lantern, it is important not to obscure the light with other masthead apparatus, such as VHF aerials or wind speed and direction transducers and brackets. Any such units fitted to the mast head must not obscure the light by more than 6° (see fig. 23). The lights have a vertical filament bulb which makes the light spread very narrow at source, so that the cut-off sectors are virtually instantaneous in order that there shall be no vague merging from one colour to another. As you can see from the foregoing points, the masthead tri-colour lantern is only recommended as an addition to the ship's lighting; because the white masthead steaming light has to be above the port and starboard and stern lights, you cannot replace the pulpit or deck lights with the tri-colour. It is nevertheless a worthwhile addition, when you realise that deck or pulpit lights are often hidden from view under some sailing conditions. The tri-colour lantern at the masthead reduces battery problems. A 25 watt bulb is visible through the coloured lens for over two miles, add two watts for a compass light and there is a battery drain of just over 2 amps, something that even a car battery can supply for at least two nights.

Glare is another important point to watch, because there is little point in fitting bright lights if they themselves prevent the crew from keeping a proper look out. Do not fit stern lights too close to the helmsman; if you cannot get them well aft of the helming position, mount them well up–this in itself will make the lights more visible to others and well above the crew's line of sight. My advice for the most seamanlike lighting set-up within the rule would be: a tri-colour masthead lantern for all coastal and offshore sailing; port, starboard and stern lights just above deck level for confined estuary sailing; and the 225°-arc white steaming light mounted well up the mast for use in combination with the pulpit and pushpit side and stern lights when under power.

The only other lights that can be fitted to the mast are not covered by the regulations, and these are:

A 360° white light which may be displayed at the mast head or in the forward rigging when anchored or moored close to navigable channels, where other craft may be on the move in the hours of darkness.

Deck lights, such as foredeck floodlights or spreader lights are the only other possible lighting additions, although the use of these at sea should be kept to a minimum for fear of ruining night vision.

Fitting Electric Lights and Wiring

When installing lights on a mast, be careful not to obscure them with any other fittings; position them clear or above the baby stay or the spinnaker topping lift exit box. Try to position the lights in such a way that they will be protected from external halyards, spreaders, the baby stay or radar reflector; radar scanner platforms and staysail boxes can offer a little protection. Ensure that the lights are lined up fore and aft on the mast; if you get them slightly out of line, you will put the colour sector angles out by the same amount.

The wires for these lights can be clipped down the outside of the mast but, for appearance, it is usually preferable to keep them inside. If they are fitted internally, they should be run in a conduit fitted in the mast, for the following reasons:

1. Wire led inside the mast by itself will rattle against the side of the tube, giving disturbed nights in a quiet anchorage.

2. If they are not run inside a special con-

duit, they are liable to be damaged by chafe from internal halyards.

You should consult your spar maker for details of the best way to fit a conduit into your particular mast, although many modern designs have a conduit extruded in. If your mast already has a conduit, there may well be a nylon messenger run through its length which will make pulling down the electrical wire a simple task. If you already have a light fitted to the mast, with the wiring in a conduit but no messenger, the easiest way to run an additional wire (always supposing that there is room in the conduit) is to detach the existing wire from the light and attach it to a thin nylon messenger line, pull it out of the conduit leaving just the nylon messenger in its place. After making the appropriate alterations to the exit slots, you can attach to the nylon messenger the two electrical cables (the original one plus the new one) and pull the two through on the one messenger line. If you have a conduit, but no wires or messenger lines running through it, you can tackle the problem in one of two ways.

1. Before removing the mast, locate and drill into the conduit where you eventually want the cable from the fitting to enter the mast, drop a short length of chain attached to a nylon messenger down the conduit and retrieve it through the exit hole at the lower end of the mast with a piece of bent wire. You can then remove the mast from the yacht and fit the lights and wiring using the messenger line to pull the wire or wires through the conduit.

2. After removing the mast from the yacht you could use an electrician's conduit feeder to push up the mast conduit either to pull down a messenger or the appropriate wire. Ensure that the conduit you fit in your mast, or the one which is already fitted, is not too large for the application, as any excess movement of the wire in the conduit will cause tapping or rattling noises to echo through the mast. If your mast maker has fitted cables for several lights or other electrical fittings, you may already have trouble identifying the six or seven similar wires leading out of the bottom of your mast. It is worth asking him to label the wires, a task which is easily done at the time, but one that could take you a lot longer to sort out on the yacht (see plate 27).

Mast Climbing Steps

With the growing popularity of this type of fitting, a little should be said about the merits of various designs that are on the market. Because of the danger of climbing masts, these fittings should fulfil certain safety factors. They should be easy to hold by hand and not be so wide or bulky that a good grip is difficult. However, they should be wide enough and have a good non-slip finish, so that the sole of a shoe or boot will not slip from the rung. They should not project too far from the side of the mast, but they should

Plate 27. A useful way of identifying the electrical wires. A number is fixed to each wire, and a label gives the key.

Plate 28. Mast steps. These designs do not give a secure foothold.

be large enough to allow the average size seaboot to be inserted comfortably. Any excess side movement could cause loss of balance. They should not have any sharp edges or corners which could cut hands, snag clothing or damage sails and halyards. They should be spaced vertically to give a comfortable reach between each rung; any overstretching between steps could cause loss of balance. I suggest that a comfortable rise between each rung is a distance between 400 and 500mm (15-20in). This spacing should be suitable for a person of average height and agility, although it could be reduced for a more aged or less mobile owner.

Having considered these criteria, climbing steps constructed of alloy or stainless steel rod or tube should be regarded as dangerous, as they do not give a wide enough bearing for a foot hold (see plate 28). Those made of wide alloy plate are also dangerous because they are too wide to get a decent hand hold and, being made of thin plate, they are hard on the fingers; this type of step often has a non-

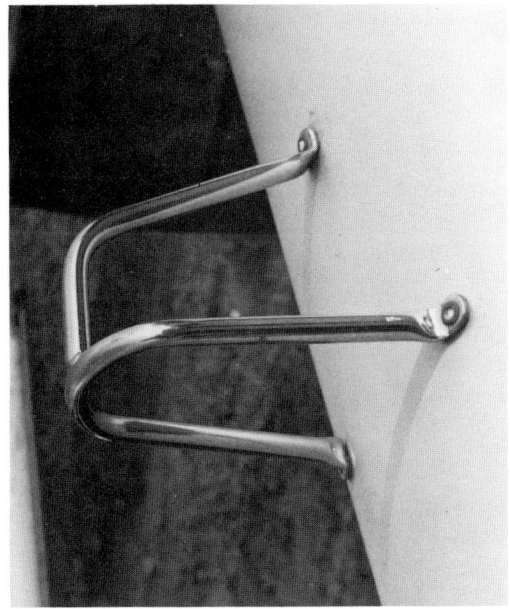

slip painted finish which in time wears off so that they become slippery and dangerous. In my opinion the type of step shown in plate 29 fulfils all the requirements. It is wide enough to prevent the shoe from slipping, it is of correct width for the average sized foot, yet not so wide that it cannot be held on to with ease. The diamond shaped patterned tread is in the alloy casting and will not wear off, giving good security. There is little to go wrong, except perhaps with the attachment points to the mast. I would suggest regular examination of each step checking for loose fastenings. At the first sign of any of the rivets working loose, they should be replaced.

Why have mast climbing steps when you can use a bosun's chair? If you sail short-handed, there may not be a crew member strong enough to winch you aloft for any repairs or maintenance that will be required during the season. Also, if you wish to go aloft whilst at sea for observation, or to repair damage to halyards or blocks, you may find yourself in the situation where there is no spare halyard available. For the cruising man, these are two good reasons for mast steps. A

Plate 29. One of the best designs of mast climbing step. Note the diamond-shaped pattern on the top of the rung which gives a good non-slip surface.

minor point to watch for is that loose halyards can get caught behind a step or steps, so extra care is needed in the dark.

Mast Lowering Devices (Tabernacles)

There are many types of fittings available to aid raising and lowering the mast. The most common type is the tabernacle, although there are several hinged shoes available. It does not really matter which type you prefer, as they all work well, though they have several limitations.

It is virtually impossible to lower the mast on a yacht over 7 metres (23 feet) in length without some form of mechanical aid. For example, if you were to use the genoa halyard to lower the mast, once the mast has reached approximately 45°, the halyard would be at a very small angle to the mast so that, though the load on it would be enormous, it would be giving the mast very little support, causing the spar to crash down to the deck out of control. It is therefore necessary to arrange a raising and lowering spar, to widen the angle between the mast and the halyard or forestay. Figure 24 shows one suggestion, using spinnaker poles to form an A-frame from the toe rail, with a fixed strop from the top of the A-frame to the stemhead fitting. If the halyard were attached to the top of this frame, the angle would be sufficiently improved for the mast to be raised and lowered by use of the genoa halyard winch. This arrangement improves the angle between the genoa halyard and mast, never allowing the angles to be reduced to the point where all support and control are lost. It is rare that the cap shrouds are attached to the chain plates at the same

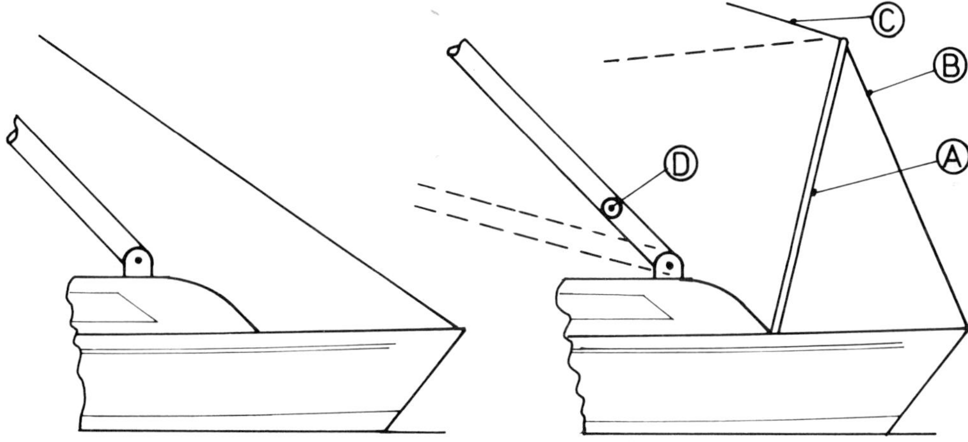

24. In the left hand view the mast has reached 45°, and the genoa halyard, which is attached to the stemhead fitting, is approaching the same angle as the mast, and will not give the required control (support angle). In the right hand view, an A-frame (A) is made from the boat's spinnaker poles, they are connected to the toe-rail on the port and starboard side, and joined to each other at the apex. B is a fixed length strop from the stemhead to the apex of the A-frame. C is the genoa halyard, which is attached to the top of the A-frame. D is the genoa winch, which is used for adjusting the genoa halyard when raising and lowering the mast.

height as the mast pivot point; because of the coach roof, they are usually positioned at a lower point. This means that, as the mast is lowered, the cap shrouds slacken as their direct line from the mast head to the chain plates is reduced. This allows the mast free movement sideways which can put undue strain on the tabernacle or heel fitting. It is essential that the mast is firmly controlled sideways, so that this free movement is prevented when lowering. If it is not possible to raise the chain plate to the mast pivot point, one suggestion is to insert a ring of suitable strength in the cap shroud horizontally adjacent to the mast pivot. This ring can be braced or guyed fore and aft when the mast is lowered, thus keeping it directly adjacent to the mast pivot. The cap shroud will then have the same tension on it, whether the mast is vertical or horizontal (see fig. 25).

There are many different ways you can add a tabernacle or hinging heel to your mast; the use of poles is just one of the more popular methods of lowering the mast. I would suggest

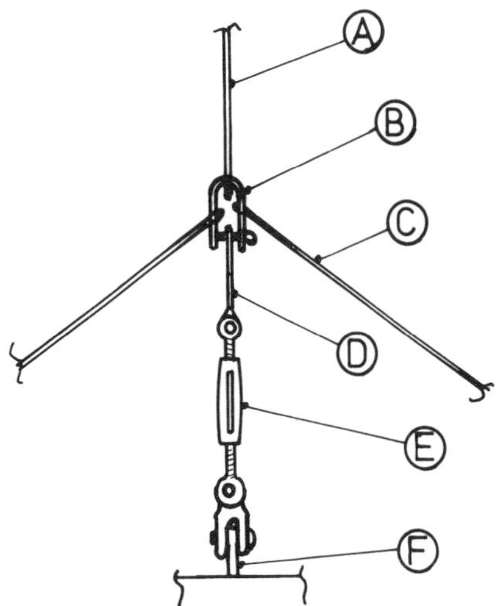

25. A: cap shroud. B: shackle, ring or toggle on horizontal pivot point of mast tabernacle. C: support guys or braces added when lowering or raising the mast. D: wire strop. E: rigging screw and toggle. F: chain plate.

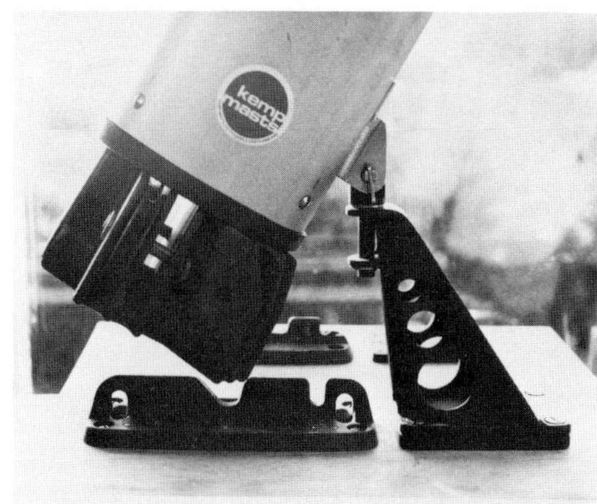

Plates 30 and 31. One way out of adding a mast lowering device to an existing heel fitting. This one can be removed from its base and stowed in a locker when not in use, and is suitable for many different types of masts and existing heel fittings.

that you contact your spar maker for further advice on the type of tabernacle or hinging heel available for your particular type of mast; he will also give you instructions on the best method of fitting it (see plates 30-33).

Kicking Strap or Vang

Whatever you prefer to call it, it is a device for improving control of the mainsail by

Plate 32. A typical mast tabernacle, where the top bolt is the pivot and the lower bolt is used for location. This type of lowering device is useful when there is a raised part of the deck or a wheelhouse directly aft of the mast. The high pivot allows the mast to lie horizontally over the obstruction.

Plate 33. Two versions of a hinged heel fitting. The low pivot bolt will only allow the mast to lie horizontally if there are no raised areas, such as a wheelhouse, directly aft of the mast.

Plate 34. A typical block and tackle kicking strap or boom vang. Simple and effective for the majority of cruisers.

restraining the boom from pivoting upwards. There are four main types:

1. handy billy or tackle system
2. lever
3. hydraulic
4. solid

The handy billy or block and tackle kicker. This is the most popular of the four, and is powerful enough for the majority of applications. It is cheap, simple, easy to adjust and normally completely trouble free. A four-part purchase is generally sufficient, although there are several types of block and tackle available which will give greater power, with more parts to the purchase, should they be required (see plate 34).

The lever kicking strap is certainly more powerful than the handy billy arrangement. It is limited by the amount of movement that can occur at the outer end of the lever. This is usually sufficient, once the position of the slider on the boom has been properly located. It is possible that if the leech cunningham flattening reef is used, the movement of the lever will not be sufficient to cover the boom both in its drooped and its horizontal positions, and it may be necessary to adjust the position of the slider on the bottom of the boom for two positions.

Hydraulic Vang. There are several types commercially available, all giving tremendous power, probably more than is really necessary. With hydraulics, it is not possible to feel when the tension is correct, and you can continue pumping without realising how much load you are putting on the boom and leech of the sail. In the hands of an over-enthusiastic

Plate 35. A lever vang or kicker. The lever is positioned in the centre of a wire strop that connects the mast swivel to the boom slide, and is adjusted by a rope tackle on the end of the lever. As the highly loaded part is wire, there is little stretch. Because of the high power of the assembly, it is advisable to fit a stop in the boom track at the most forward position of the slider, as the locking screws on the slider are only a light location to finalise position.

crew member, it is capable of breaking the boom or ripping the mainsail. It is thus important to fit a gauge for these units. Because of the higher loads generally associated with this type of fitting, it is not normally sufficient to use a locking screw to hold the slider in the boom track. It is advisable to fit a stop forward of the slider once this

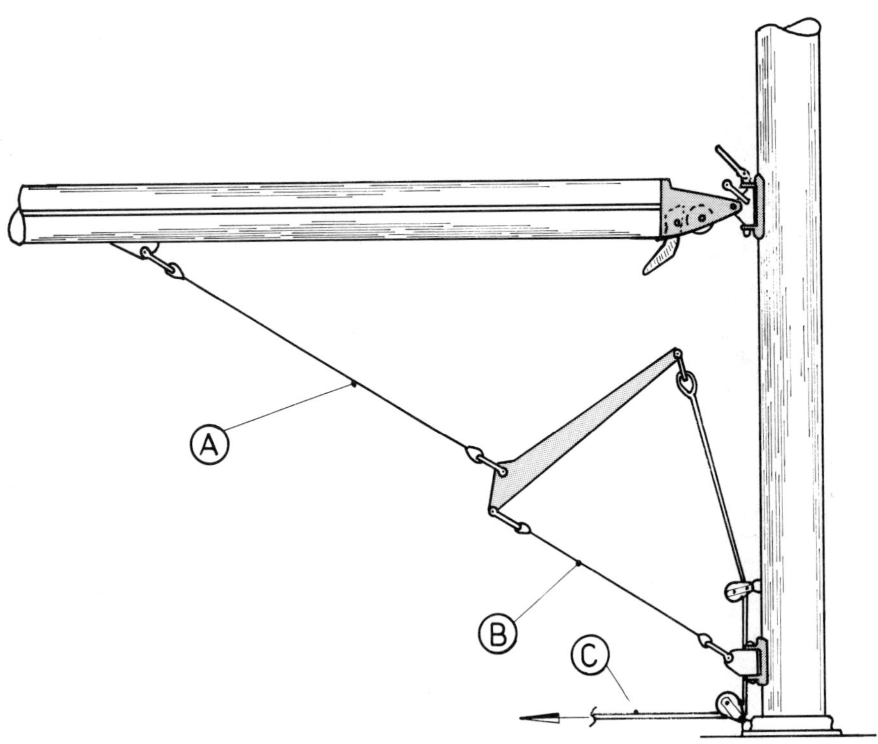

26. Kicker or vang lever assembly. A: fixed length wire strop shackles to boom slide and lever. B: fixed length wire strop shackles to lever and kicker swivel. C: adjustment rope shackled to lever. Rope must pass through a block above the kicker swivel so as to keep lever vertical.

position has been finalised. If this is not done, the locating screw could tear a slot along the aluminium track, or indeed the screw itself may shear. It is also a good idea to fit a stop 100mm (4in) aft of the slider; this serves as a 'topping lift', so that when the mainsail is lowered, the slider in the boom will move to the aft stop and then stop the boom from drooping further into the cockpit. This can dispense with the need for a main boom topping lift (see plate 36).

Plate 36. A hydraulic vang, primarily used on racing yachts.

Solid kickers offer similar power and the zero stretch properties to the hydraulic unit, and are, of course, a lot cheaper. The problem is that they are a lot slower to operate, although many of these problems can be overcome by careful positioning of boom stops, and a little forethought before use. Solid vangs are really over-size rigging screws or turnbuckles, and are adjusted by being wound in or out, usually with the help of a turning bar. You can reach a stage when you are not sure whether the vang is pulling or pushing. To overcome this problem it is recommended that two stops be fitted to the boom track so that, when the

Plate 37. Solid vang kicking strap. Note that it is attached to the mid-point of the boom, further out than is usual with other systems. This is because the nil stretch of the system means that the kicker will be effective at a much lower angle to the boom. Attaching it further out reduces the boom bend and mainsheet load, because the mainsheet has only to control the angle of the boom to the centreline of the boat, and the leech tension. On this Quarter Tonner, a simple 2 to 1 mainsheet was practicable. Note the two-sheet system; only the weather one is used at any one time, but the system can still be self-tacking if the leeward sheet is adjusted correctly.

Plate 38. Solid vang kicking strap. Note white lines on the boom so that the crew can see if the kicker is pushing, pulling or slack. The lines mark the position of the solid stops. Photo: Peter Cartwright.

slider is positioned between them, it has approximately 150mm (6in) of free movement. Thus when the vang is slackened, as soon as the load reaches zero, the slider will start to move away from the forward stop. As mentioned before, their drawback is slowness of adjustment. This is particularly apparent when slab reefing. During this operation it becomes necessary to free off the kicking strap completely. This is not generally possible with a solid one unless some form of quick release mechanism is available, or it is taken off the boom slider. Usually the vang has to be unwound until it reaches its aftermost position of travel, and then the boom will be able to rise enough to perform the reefing operation. Once the reefing is completed, the vang has to be tightened up again–a long, slow process, which brings the boom slider back to the forward position and then starts to exert force on the leech of the sail to remove the twist. Another advantage of the two stop system is that, as with the hydraulic kicker, there is no need for a main boom topping lift (see plates 37 and 38). Any kicker or vang on a boat with a tendency to broach has to have this ability to be freed quickly, if the boom is to be allowed to sky and thus dump wind from the mainsail so that control may be regained.

Plate 39. A roller box that leads the halyard out of the mast and down to the cleat, winch or deck. There is a roller inside the mast that cannot be seen. Note the round and small hole required for this fitting.

Positioning of Mast Fittings

By far the most important point to bear in mind when positioning fittings on the mast is the weakening effect of a cluster of fittings around the spar at the same level. Space them out as much as possible, especially those that require slots cut through the mast wall. Any removal of material reduces the strength of the section in that area, and the closer each of these weak areas are to each other, the more chance there will be of mast failure. Never congregate fittings in one area, even if they are only screwed or riveted to the mast wall. Even a line of rivets or screws round the mast at the same level will invite failure on the 'tear along the dotted line' principle.

When making cut-outs in the mast for exit boxes or other fittings, make sure that these holes have well-rounded corners; never cut a

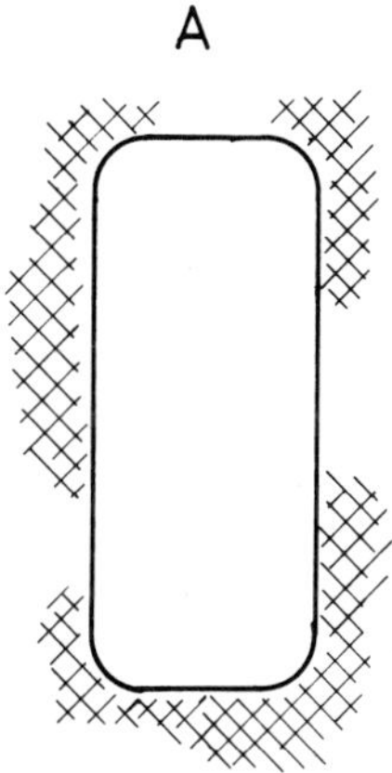

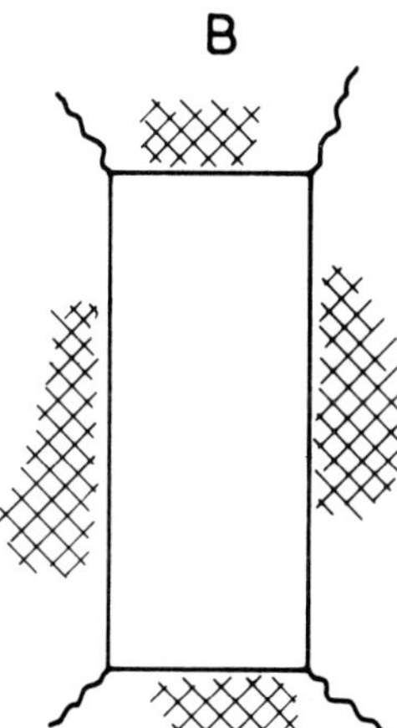

27. Cut-outs. A: all cut-outs in the mast should have well-rounded corners to avoid areas of stress concentration. B: slot with square corners, from which cracks will readily radiate.

slot with a right-angled corner, as this encourages cracks to form (see fig. 27). Always stagger these slots: never have two in the same peripheral line. Some halyard exit box fittings that can be purchased are made with square inserts. It can sometimes be difficult to fit these correctly, as there is no room to elongate the slot and round off the corner, because of the need to leave sufficient material to fasten into: nor is it possible to round the corners of the box prior to cutting the slot, as the material is not thick enough to allow you to do so. Even if it were feasible to extend the slot and round off the corners, this may not be advisable as most exit boxes (not roller boxes) rely on the fact that the insert bears against the alloy mast wall to give it its strength. If it were not bearing correctly, it would rely totally on the fastenings which, in the case of a genoa halyard, would be totally inadequate.

You would be well advised to look carefully at any fitting that has to be let into the mast wall before you purchase it, to make sure that the part that goes into the mast wall is well-rounded, not square. If you see cracks radiating from a fitting or cut-out, consult your mast maker immediately. If it is impossible to seek expert advice, drill a hole about 6 or 8mm diameter ($\frac{1}{4}$in or 5/16in) at the end of the crack, not at the place where the crack has started, but at the place where

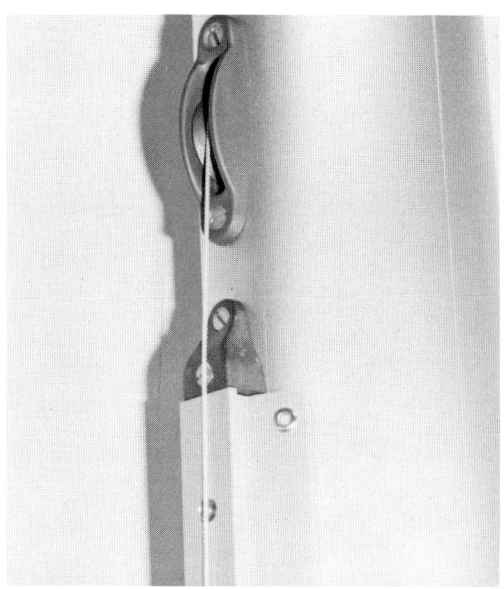

Plate 40. An exit box that turns the halyard 180°, bringing it up to a cleat or winch from the bottom of the mast or, as illustrated, being used for the spinnaker pole heel lift halyard. This fitting has a larger cut-out than the roller box. The important thing is to keep the width of the slot to a minimum, and give it a full radius at the top and bottom ends. Note rounded top and bottom of fitting.

the crack has reached; this will temporarily halt its progress. How temporary this will be depends very much on the severity and location of the crack. You would be wise to reduce the loads in the rig during any further sailing until the problem is dealt with. The best way to reduce rigging load is to sail with 10° less heel than normal and bear off 10° from the wind when beating to windward. This will take you a lot longer to get home, but at least you may arrive in one piece. After having identified and dealt with the crack as above, keep up a regular check during further sailing. At the first sign of it extending beyond the drilled hole, reduce sail and speed still further, as there is clearly a major problem. After all, you are better placed to limp home with the mast still intact than you would be without it.

seven

Mainsail Luff Control

There are two principal ways of attaching the mainsail to the mast: by a mainsail luff rope or with sail slides. Within these two categories there are several variations. There is no right or wrong way of doing this, as each method has its own merits, depending on the type of reefing system to be used, the type of sailing to be undertaken and the number of crew who will be available on the boat.

Luff Rope

This is the system whereby a rope is attached to the length of the mainsail luff and is then fed directly into the groove on the back of the mast. This system is preferred by the racing enthusiast who requires a quick slab reefing adjustment and has the crew to handle it. There is also a dedicated band of cruiser/racer owners who use this system with through-mast reefing (see Chapter 8). Using this gear, the boom can be rotated very quickly, so that the mainsail can be completely furled around the boom by one or two persons when approaching harbour, or it is very quick to put in two or three turns of the boom when racing, although it seems generally accepted that the mainsail does not have such a good set with through-mast reefing as it has with a slab system.

The disadvantage of the luff rope (except with through-mast reefing), is the inability to control the sail when reefing or lowering the mainsail. This is because it has to come right off the mast as it is lowered. Imagine coming to the entrance of a congested marina when short-handed: you go forward to lower the mainsail, release the halyard and drop the sail on deck, but, before you have had time to secure the halyard tail, a gust of wind has blown the mainsail off the deck and up into the air. You are now heading into the berthing area at an increasing speed, with the mainsail set like a spinnaker on a long halyard out to leeward. For whichever reason you decide that luff rope is right for you, the important thing is that the sail must feed easily into the mast. If you have ever tried hoisting a groove luff mainsail, you will realise how easily it can jam in the opening. All sorts of fairings and lead-in fittings have been tried, but none that I have seen has ever totally overcome this problem. The manufacturers of plastic and alloy genoa luff grooves found the same problems, and they have overcome it with various systems of pre-feeders. You will never see a genoa head foil where the genoa feeds directly into the groove; they are always given a fair line into the groove by the use of a pre-feeder. Mainsails are no different, they also have to be given the correct line into the groove. Plate 41 shows such a pre-feeder fitted below the groove entry fitting.

Sail Slides

The use of sail slides is an older method of

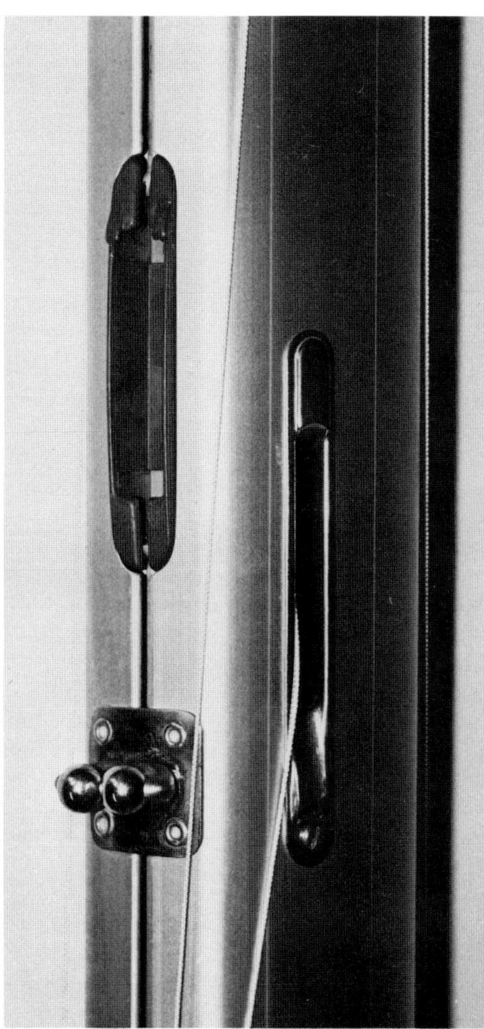

attaching the mainsail to the mast, and in my opinion is the most seamanlike. Sail slides have two principal advantages: they reduce the amount of wear and tear on the luff of the mainsail and when the sail is lowered, they hold it to the mast; as pointed out earlier in this chapter, this is a great advantage when sailing short-handed. Sail slides should always run freely in the mast groove or track. I know that a lot of owners have been put off because they have had bad experience of slides not running freely up and down in the mast groove or track. There are usually very straightforward reasons for this, although some of them may not be very obvious.

Metal slides of any sort should never be used on alloy masts, as they will have high friction and, in time, will score the track and cause corrosion, which will only make the situation progressively worse. Always use nylon or nylon composite slides. Nylon is an inert material which is water lubricated (so don't grease them) and will not score or damage the mast groove or track. Check with your mast maker to see if the correct slides have been fitted to your mainsail. There are several alternatives on the market for every

Plate 41. Mainsail luff rope entry and pre-feeder. Shown just a short distance below the mainsail groove entry is the pre-feeder. It has two balls that are free to turn, and they guide the luff rope into the correct alignment for feeding into the mast groove, and thus minimise jamming. The fitting shown on the side of the mast is a halyard exit slot; note the well-rounded guides and fairing that will reduce halyard wear.

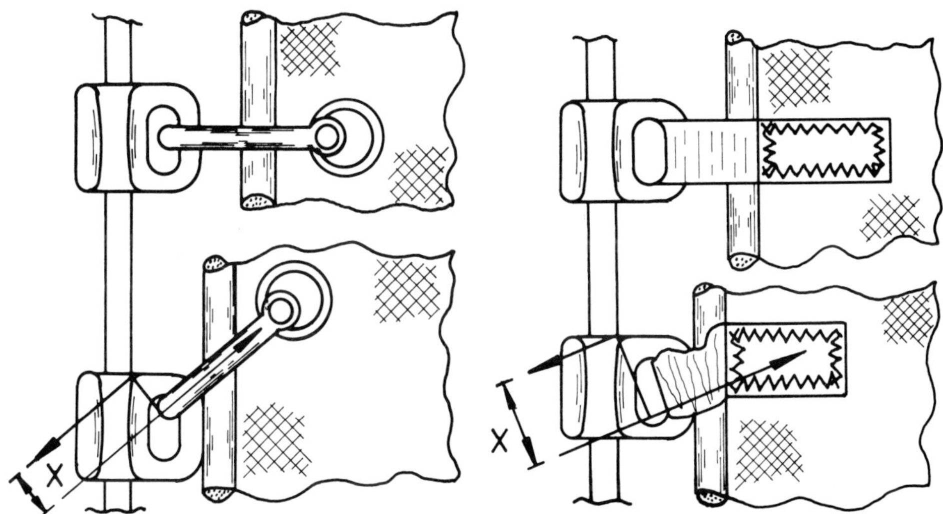

28. Attaching slides to the sail. Left: the correct method, using a round shackle that can move freely in the sail slide. It is the distance marked X which is crucial: if it is kept small, there is only a small turning moment on the slide, and it runs freely. Right: the sail incorrectly attached, by means of a fabric band or wide shackle; here distance X is too great, and the slide will jam.

design of track and groove; inevitably some will appear to fit correctly but will have certain less obvious features which will make them less than satisfactory in application. When you have the correct sail slide for the mast groove, make sure it is fitted to the mainsail correctly; slides fitted to the sail with a fabric band or wide shackle will twist and jam regularly. To avoid this twisting and jamming in the mast groove, the slides should be fastened to the sail by a nylon shackle that is round and free to move in the slide. This will decrease the leverage on the slide, and so decrease the tendency to twist and jam (see fig. 28). When using sail slides with slab reefing, ensure that the sail slides are not fitted close to or adjacent to the reef cringle.

If they are, you will have to remove the slides from the mast every time you wish to reef. Have the sail slides fitted so that the reefing cringle is appropriately placed somewhere between the two slides; in this way the first and sometimes the second reef (the most-used reefs) can be made without removing

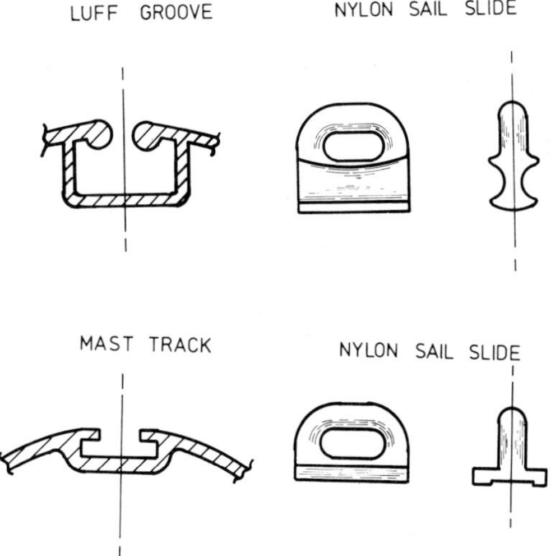

29. Top: luff groove, showing a typical nylon sail slide for a groove. The aft face of the sail slide should be well rounded to prevent the top corner catching the mast groove and jamming. Bottom: mast track and typical nylon slide. The aft face of the slide should be parallel to the forward side so that, because of the close fore and aft fit, it cannot turn and jam in the mast track.

the slides from the mast. This means that the cringle is free to be fitted to the tack hooks, as it is not being restrained because of the close proximity of a sail slide. It is only the build-up of slides between the boom and second reef cringle that may prevent the cringle reaching down to the tack hooks; this will depend on the depth of the reefs and the spacing of the sail slides.

Track Gates

For the two types of sail slide shown in fig. 29, two completely different gate systems have to be used. For the mast track type of system, part of the outer flange of the track has to be removed. This has to be replaced with a metal plate that can be made removable by means of an adjustable locking screw. Usually it is necessary to remove only one of the outer flanges so that the sail slide comes out with a twisting action (see plate 42). The second type of gate is for a sail slide which is used in a luff groove; this is completely different in its approach, and is illustrated in fig. 30. The centre part of this gate is spring loaded so that it always returns to the position that allows the slide to pass the gate and rest directly above the boom. When using a luff rope (bolt rope) instead of sail slides, only the outer part of the gate illustrated for the groove slides is used. With this type of arrangement, it is essential to have a pre-feeder in front of this entry point (see plate 41). If this type of pre-feeder is not used, the rope has a tendency to jam in the entry.

Trysails and Tracks

It is quite possible, and often accepted, that a trysail can be fitted in the mast track above the stowed mainsail. This is probably easier in theory than it is in practice. When trysails are used, conditions are bad and deteriorating,

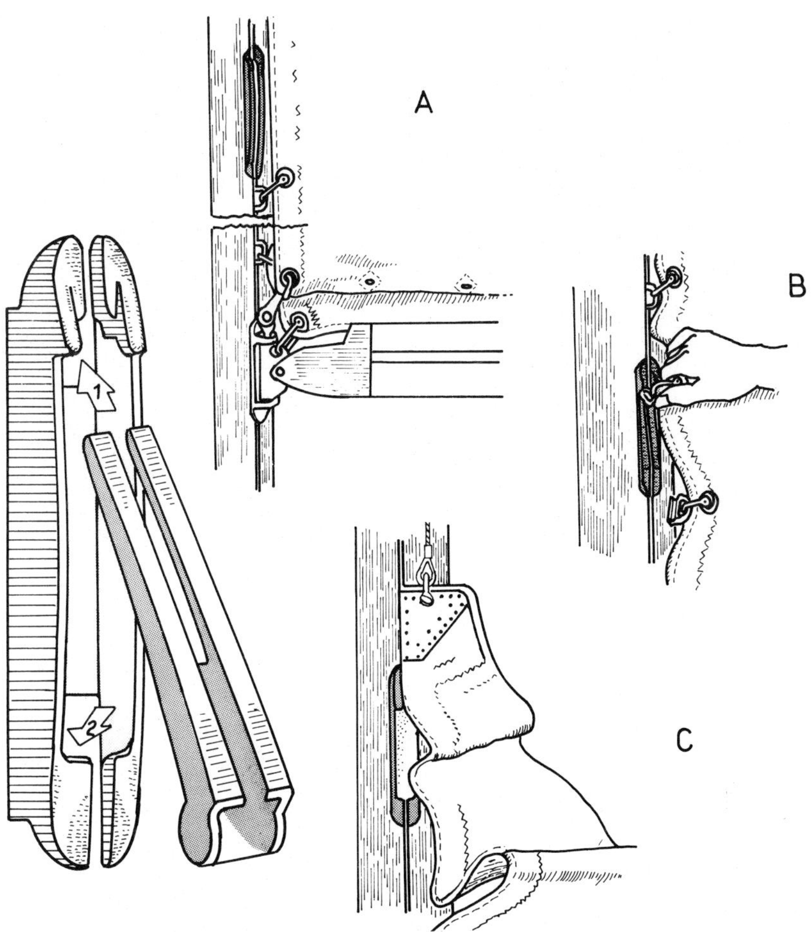

30. Track gate for luff rope and slides. A: when stowing the sail or making the first reef, the slides need not be taken out of the groove, as they are able to pass through the closed gate down to boom level. The advantage is that the sail is never free of the mast, making faster and safer reefing. B: the centre part of the gate springs down when the slides are fed in. C: when the centre part of the gate is removed, the outer part is a sail feeder for luff-roped mainsails.

Plate 42. Track Gate for internal track. Left: track gate in place allows the sail slide to pass to boom level. Right: the sail slide twists to come out of the gate when the lock screw is released and the gate is swung clear.

and it is not very easy to take the trysail and fit it above the stowed main. It is far easier to fit it in a separate track that runs below the boom to deck level. These tracks are positioned on the aft quarter of the mast and run from spreader height to deck level. The trysail can then be flaked out along the deck of the boat and fitted in to the track at deck level.

Sail Slide Maintenance

Salt crystals and dirt build-up will in time reduce the free running of sail slides. It is important to wash out the track twice yearly and apply a coat of silicone wax polish; this will help keep friction to a minimum, and provide a protection for the track and alloy spar. Any grease which is used will inevitably get onto the sails, so this is another reason for preferring nylon slides; they should be of the internal type, or they will not be strong enough.

eight

Booms and Reefing Systems

There are two main systems of reefing. The first is roller reefing, where the boom is rotated so that the sail is wound round the boom to reduce area progressively. The second is slab reefing, where a pre-determined area is reduced in one operation by means of pulling a new tack and a new clew cringle down to the top of the boom; the sail is reduced by the area bounded by the old and new tack and clew cringles. Of the two, slab, or jiffy reefing as it is also called, gives a better setting mainsail, because a roller boom does not correctly control the shape of the foot of the sail.

Plate 43. A typical worm screw roller reefing gear.

Roller Reefing

There are two main types of roller reefing. First, worm reefing gear, of which a good example is the Gibb worm gear shown in plate 43. This system has been used for a great number of years and has many protagonists. Apart from the old-fashioned lacing reefing, it is probably the slowest of all the reefing methods, but has certain advantages over others. When sailing short-handed, there is only one operation to perform at a time. As you rotate the boom and reduce canvas, the gooseneck runs up the mast track, so it is not necessary to pay out the halyard at the same time as turning the reefing handle. Because it is a worm gear, you can leave the reefing operation at any time to attend to other

Plate 44. Worm gear roller reefing. Left top: assembled reefing gear. Right top: removal of gear housing showing the gear wheel that is fixed to the boom. Left bottom: gear wheel shown pinned to the boom fitting. Right bottom: shows worm screw that is captive in the gear housing.

Plate 45. A typical through-mast reefing gear. Note how the handle locks and stows vertically down mast.

problems which may occur, and later return to the interrupted reefing operation.

For those unfamiliar with it, a worm gear operates with only two moving parts (see plate 44). A gear wheel attached to the boom has teeth inclined at a small angle; it is engaged by a large screw thread which is rotated by the reefing handle. A suitable housing ensures that turning the reefing handle rotates the boom without causing the screw thread to travel in or out. Because of the mechanical advantage (typically twelve

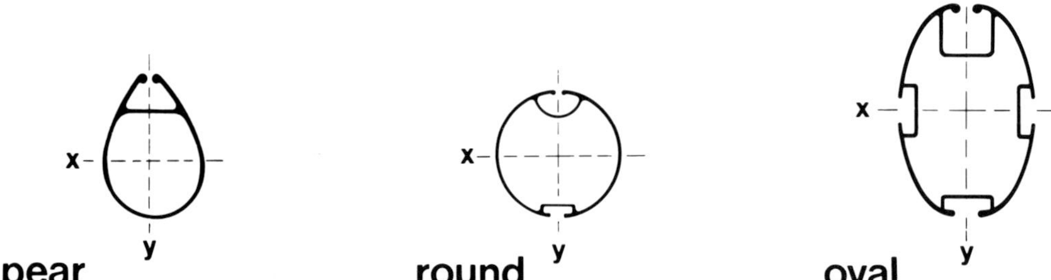

31. Boom sections. Left: pear-shaped booms are little used today, except on mizzen booms, which do not normally require any form of reefing. Middle: round booms are suitable for any form of roller reefing. The boom has a similar strength in all axes, and can therefore be used with its vertical axis Y in any direction after reefing. Right: slab-reefing boom with tracks on the underside for the kicker or vang, and in the side for reefing slides. As the boom is never turned and always working in the same plane, it does not require the same side strength (inertia).

turns of the handle for one turn of the boom) and the angle which the screw thread makes with the gear wheel, it is not possible for the boom to drive the handle, which is why the reefing operation may be left at any stage and why no locking mechanism is used.

The second roller reefing system is the through-mast type. This is usually a direct drive and thus much faster than the worm gear system; so quick is it that, when coming into harbour, crews often prefer to furl the mainsail by rolling it round the boom. The disadvantages for reefing are that two simultaneous operations are required. Because the reefing handle is connected from the front of the mast straight through to the boom (see plate 45), it follows that the gooseneck will not be able to travel up the mast as the handle is turned. Therefore the main halyard has to be eased as the reef is taken in. The other disadvantage is that the handle will only lock off in one position, so a full 360° roll of the boom must be completed before you can leave reefing to attend to any other problems.

The best type of boom section to use with any form of roller reefing is a round one. The sail will run more kindly on a round section and, more important, the boom has similar strength in all directions so, if a reefing operation is only partially completed, i.e. if axis Y (see fig. 31) were horizontal rather than vertical, the boom would be just as strong and safe as it would have been had axis Y been vertical. To enlarge on that statement, you must appreciate that a boom requires more vertical strength than horizontal strength. The forces imposed by the kicking strap or boom vang, the sail clew and, to a lesser extent, the mainsheet, are all acting in the vertical plane. There are only the relatively low compressive forces (wrapping of the boom round the shrouds during uncontrolled gybes, or the occasional dunking of the boom in the sea) that put any side loading on the boom. If it were not for the roller reefing feature, the side strength of a main boom could be reduced by fifty per cent of the vertical strength–indeed it often is, where slab reefing is employed. One of the biggest disadvantages with any form of roller reefing is the problem of using a kicking strap or centre main sheet whilst the sail is wound round the boom. Various ways are used to overcome this problem, although none of them offers a perfect solution. The claw ring fits round the boom so that reefs can be rolled down between the boom and ring, but the wheels on the top of the claw bear hard on the sail causing excessive wear (see plate 46). Winding a webbing strap round the boom as the sail is rolled down is another trick which is a lot kinder on the mainsail, but it is a real problem to wind it in under difficult conditions, particularly when sailing short-handed.

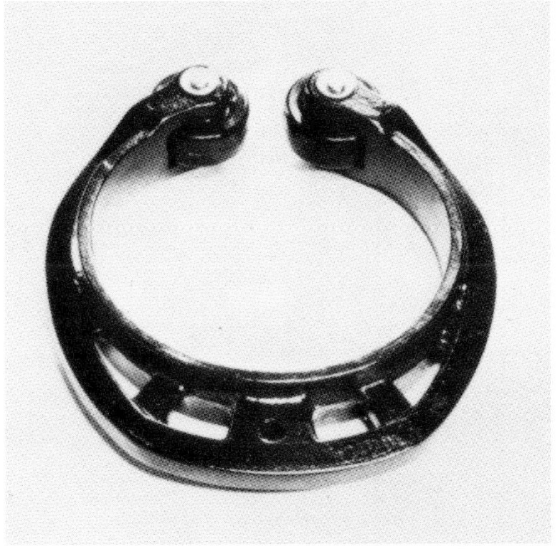

Plate 46. Claw ring. Used on booms for mainsheet and kicking strap attachments when roller reefing.

Slab Reefing

Booms used with slab reefing systems are generally oval in section, as it is not necessary for the boom to have the same strength in all directions. The popularity of this type of reefing probably stems from the continent, particularly France. Booms which they started producing several years ago were developed from the old-fashioned wooden booms before the Second World War and are, by today's standards, cumbersome and awkward in operation. They usually had the reef lines running through cheek blocks on the side of the boom and invariably had the winches mounted on the boom itself. Gear developed in Britain for racing boats gives a system which is now suitable for the demands of the

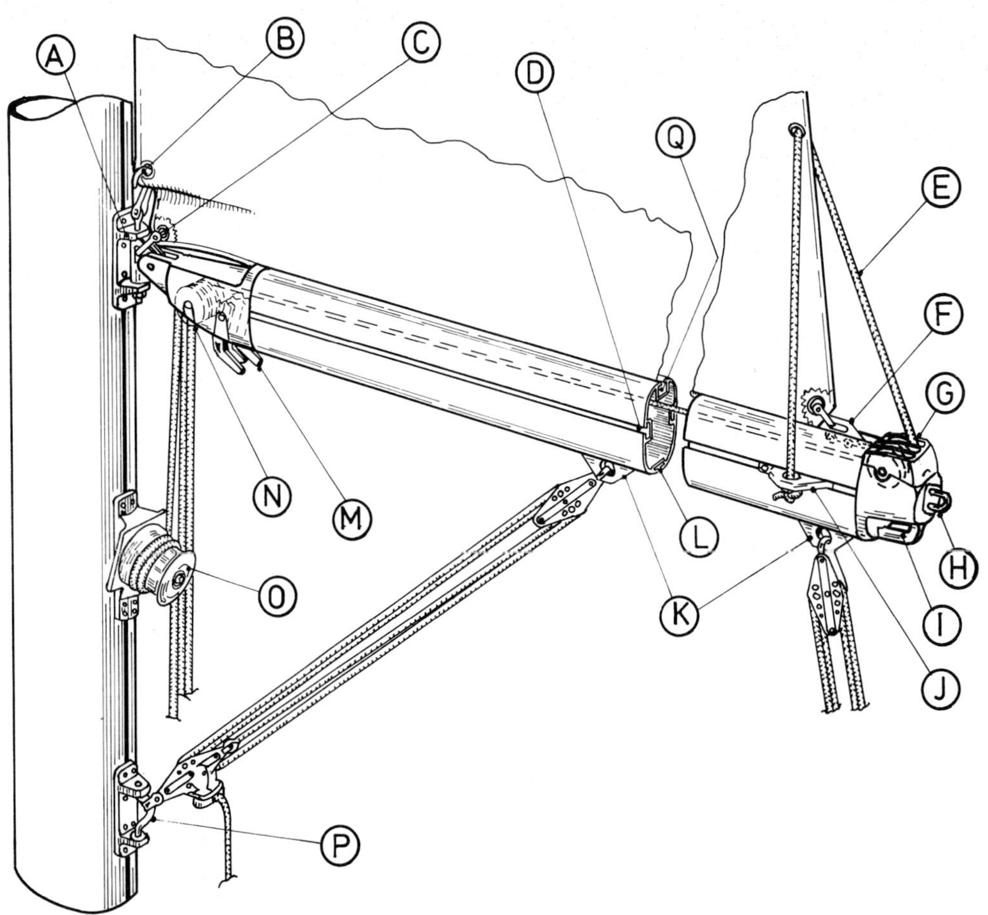

32. Slab-reefing boom. A: fixed gooseneck bracket so that boom height cannot be affected by tension in reefing line E when used on winch O. B: tack hook close to mast to reduce mainsail creasing when reefed. C: tack shackle. D: grooves on port and starboard sides of boom for adjustable clew reefing slides J. E: clew reefing line. F: clew car to take tension in leech of mainsail. G: three sheaves for controlling outhaul and reefing lines and to lead ropes internally to sheaves (N) and jam levers (M). H: main boom topping lift eye. I: alternative mainsheet take-off point. J: adjustable clew reefing slide (two for each reef position). K: kicking strap or vang and mainsheet adjustable slides. L: track in bottom of boom for kicker vang and mainsheet slides K. M: three jam levers for the three internal clew lines. As the lines are jammed individually on the boom, winch O is always free for the next reefing operation. N: three sheaves to lead clew lines down to winch O. O: clew line winch mounted at an angle to prevent riding turns. P: kicking strap swivel on fixed backing plate. Q: groove in top of boom for mainsail foot rope and clew car F.

racing enthusiast and, because of its simplicity of operation, is becoming increasingly popular both with the family cruising man and the deep sea, long distance sailor. Figure 32 shows the set up. The advantage with this system is that the reef lines are internal, there are no winches or mechanical aids mounted on the boom and, unlike roller reefing booms, the kicking strap can be used when reefed. For the racing man, the clew control lines can be taken aft to cockpit winches, whereas the family cruising man can use the winch mounted on the aft side of the mast, as in fig. 32. When racing, there is little problem in reefing quickly with enough crew members on board to attend to all the necessary tasks. When short-handed sailing, the operation will naturally take longer to perform, and a standard procedure should be adopted every time you reef, so that the task does not get out of hand:

1. Slack off or remove the kicking strap or boom vang.
2. Make off the main boom topping lift so that the boom will not drop when the main halyard is released, and hit crew members in the cockpit. Alternatively set up a solid vang so the boom is held horizontal.
3. Lower the main halyard until the appropriate tack reef cringle is adjacent to the gooseneck.
4. Slip the tack reef cringle on to the hooks at the gooseneck and tighten up the main halyard as required.
5. Release the mainsheet.
6. Pull in on the appropriate clew line with one or two turns around the reefing winch. Having released the kicking strap and mainsheet, you will find that the outer end of the boom will rise to the appropriate cringle. When the cringle is close to the boom, you will have to winch in the remainder to get correct foot tension.
7. Jam the appropriate clew line with the locking lever by the gooseneck. This frees the winch for another operation and subsequent reefs that may be required.
8. Slacken off the main topping lift.
9. Tighten the mainsheet.
10. Make off the kicking strap.
11. Tidy up the bag of the mainsail and the reef lines if desired. This should now see the successful conclusion of the reefing operation.

On the sketch of a slab reefing boom, there is only one clew slider (J) illustrated. Ideally, a slider is useful on both port and starboard sides of the boom for each reefing operation. Sliders are fitted at the appropriate fore and aft positions on the boom for each reef line on the mainsail. This position is determined by the cut of the mainsail, and how much foot tension is required when the sail is reefed. As the reefing line E is always going to the sheaves in position G, it produces a large aft component, and it follows that to reduce foot tension, the reefing slider J may have to be positioned forward of the reef cringle. Figure 33 shows the slider positioned aft of the reef cringle, and illustrates the resultant force caused by

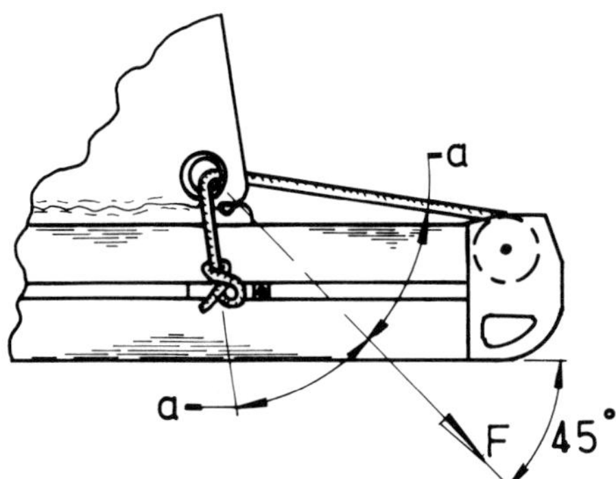

33. Positioning clew slides. Resultant force F should be at 45° to the underside of the boom when the angles a *are equal. The angle of 45° may be adjusted by the slides in the side track so that, for example, moving the slides forward increases the angle above 45°, putting less load on the foot of the mainsail.*

such positioning. The slide positioning becomes even more important with deep reefs as the first reef is only a short distance from the sheaves G, the reefing slider J will only be adjacent to the reef cringle; but on the second and third reefs, the cringle comes further along the boom, and the slider has to be positioned progressively further forward along the boom to compensate for this. After the position of the clew slider has been determined, the boom should be drilled so that the locating screw enters this hole and makes a secure and positive location, so as to avoid the possibility of the slider slipping along the boom when in use.

It was mentioned earlier that two sliders are ideal for each reef, one port and one starboard; this is advisable so that the reefing operation is not restricted to one side of the boom. In theory, it is only necessary to have one of these, but in practice it is not always convenient if the slider is on the lee side of the boom, which is more difficult to work from in rough conditions. It is best, once the position of the slide has been finalised, to fit another one directly opposite.

The mainsail foot has all the working loads taken on the tack and clew. This can be illustrated by the fact that the reef is only held at these two points, and the bag of the sail between them is gathered to the boom for neatness only. The same applies when the full mainsail is set; it is only the tack and clew which take the load, and the sail between these points is retained at the boom by a foot rope: there is little vertical load between these two points. The tack of the mainsail is held down to the boom at the gooseneck end by a shackle, but the highly loaded clew end of the sail relies upon the bolt rope sewn to the foot for its retention in the groove. When this is the case, a lot of wear occurs at this point and the mainsail will need frequent repairs. It is also possible that this rope may distort or pull out and jam in the boom groove. The most seamanlike and structurally correct answer is for the leech of the sail to be secured to a clew car (see letter F in fig. 32) which will take all of the necessary load and prevent this problem; otherwise take a lashing round the boom and through the clew eye. Where slides are used along the foot, have one on the clew eye itself if no clew car is fitted.

With the type of reefing system shown in figure 32, it is not always necessary to have an internal outhaul, as there are three lines at the outer end of the boom, and only one line is in use at any one time. Therefore one of the lines not in use can be used as a foot outhaul, and once the leech flattener or first reef has been pulled down, the line originally used for the outhaul can be freed for further applications. This is made possible because the winch on the aft side of the mast gives plenty of power for this operation, thus doing away with the block and tackle type of outhaul inside the boom. This latter system has a reputation for going wrong anyway: they can easily twist and become useless, and then the boom has to be dismantled for inspection and repair. On roller reefing booms, however, the winch on the aft side of the mast is not available, and the block and tackle method on the inside of the boom has to be adopted. To avoid the twisting problems with this type of tackle, it is advisable to have the static block (i.e. the forward block) positioned in the boom so that it is not free to turn over; this halves the chance of having a capsized block. It is not normally possible to have the moving block at the outer end of the boom positioned so that it cannot turn over, but halving the chances of a snarl-up will certainly help. Generally speaking, a three- or four-part tackle will be sufficient for this operation. As these outhauls are mostly used on roller reefing booms, it is important that the jamming mechanism for them is contained inside the boom, or at least is flush with the outer face; any protrusion will do damage to the mainsail when it is tightly wound around the boom.

Maintenance

Worm gear: situated on the gear box housing are oiling points. The gears should be well lubricated with a light machine oil three or four times in a season. Keep all other exterior moving parts lubricated and free from salt by use of an aerosol lubricant.

Through mast gear: the direct drive mechanism requires little maintenance, apart from ensuring that it is kept free from salt water crystals and that bearings and any other moving parts are kept lubricated with the aersol.

Slab reefing: as with all sheaves mentioned earlier in this book, make sure that they are kept free running and free from salt crystals. Regular lubrication with the aerosol is essential; spray on lightly and clean all moving parts on this type of boom.

nine

Spinnaker Control Systems

Spinnaker End Fittings

In mechanical terms, there are two types of fitting: end opening and top opening, the latter including the trip trigger fitting.

The end opening type is suitable, and principally designed, for end-for-end gybing systems, whereas top opening fittings are suitable for dip-pole or double-pole gybing systems. However, either type can be used for the other system.

End-for-End Gybing

On yachts up to 7·5 metres overall (24ft 6in), end-for-end gybing with single sheet and guy is probably the most suitable system available (see fig. 34). On yachts up to 11 metres overall length (36ft), it is still simpler and easier to use an end-for-end gybing system, but with some modifications: it is essential to use a double sheet and guy system (see fig. 35). This means that the whole operation can be completed without having to fight the sail. As can be seen, the pole is brought across the

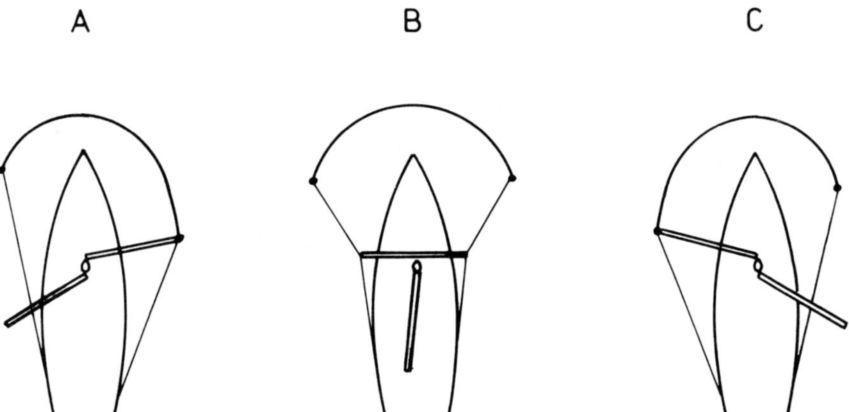

34. End-for-end gybe with single sheet and guy or brace. A: pole is removed from ring on mast. B: the pole is moved across the yacht, and the end that has just been removed from the mast ring is now connected to the port side sheet. C: the starboard sheet is released and the pole connected to the mast. Note that the sheet being released (starboard side) from the pole is deflected, and when the plunger is released it will try to regain a straight line from the spinnaker clew to deck block; this means sideways movement, which the end-opening pole allows. The top-opening type restricts movement so, if this type of pole is used, it will have to be dipped, or the starboard sheet lifted out of the fitting.

boat and put on the new side with only the handling weight of the pole. With this system, as with dip-pole gybing (see below), there is a period of time when the spinnaker is held by the sheet and guy alone, and the pole therefore does not have a stabilising influence. To overcome this problem it is recommended that the spare sheet and guy be led well forward. This stops the spinnaker lifting, and gives a shorter length of rope between the fastening point on the boat and the clew of the spinnaker, so that the sail has less chance of movement.

Dip-Pole Gybing

This is mainly used on yachts over 11 metres (36ft) overall, when the dead weight of the spinnaker pole and its equipment is too much for easy manhandling on the foredeck, and end-for-ending is not practical. However, in all other respects, it has the same limitations as end-for-ending. You have to use a spare sheet and guy attached well forward on the yacht, to stabilise the spinnaker when it is free of the pole during the gybe (see fig. 36).

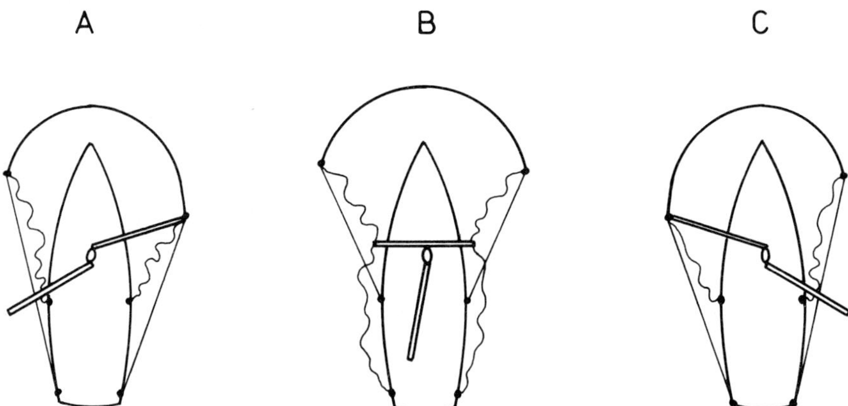

35. End-for-end gybe with double sheets and guys or braces. A: load is taken by the lazy sheet and guy, then the original (aft guy or brace) is released; the pole is removed from the mast ring. B: the pole is moved across the boat and connected to the sheet that is not in use; the starboard lazy sheet is released from the pole end. C: the pole is connected to the mast; you can then take the spinnaker load back on the aft sheet (starboard side) to allow the clew to rise to the same height as the corner of the spinnaker that is attached to the pole. Note that the sheet being released from the pole end has no weight on it, and will be easier to remove from the pole on the end-opening fitting.

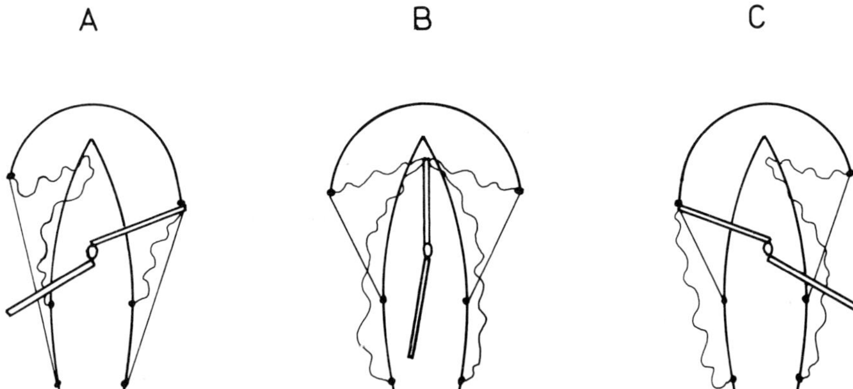

36. Dip-pole gybe (double sheets and after guys or braces are essential). A: the port side lazy sheet is led forward to the forestay tack; the load is taken on the starboard side lazy after guy. B: the pole is pulled forward and simultaneously lowered under the forestay with the old, now redundant, brace or guy still attached. The redundant (starboard) brace or guy is removed from the pole end fitting and the new (port) lazy brace or guy put into the pole end fitting. C: the pole can now be pulled aft and raised to required height with the new guy or brace attached. Take the guy load onto the line that is in the pole end and, release the now redundant port side line that is not through the pole end fitting. You may now take the load back on to the aft starboard sheet if required.

Double-Pole Gybing

This is used as an alternative to the dip-pole system and has the advantage that there is always a pole in position throughout the operation. This in itself makes the spinnaker considerably more controllable, but it does double the amount of equipment necessary to gybe the sail. However, most yachts of this size have enough crew on board to cope with the extra work, and often the added security of this procedure makes it an attractive proposition (see fig. 37). As you have probably seen from diagrams illustrating the various gybing systems, the end-opening type of pole fitting is far better for end-for-end gybing, as it is always necessary for the old guy to come out of the pole end in a horizontal direction. It is also easier to connect the new guy in the same plane, and connection to the ring is easier from the end of the pole rather than the top (see plate 47). The top-opening type of fitting is more suited to the dip-pole and double-pole gybe: as can be seen from the illustration, the guy is always trying to come out of the pole in an upward

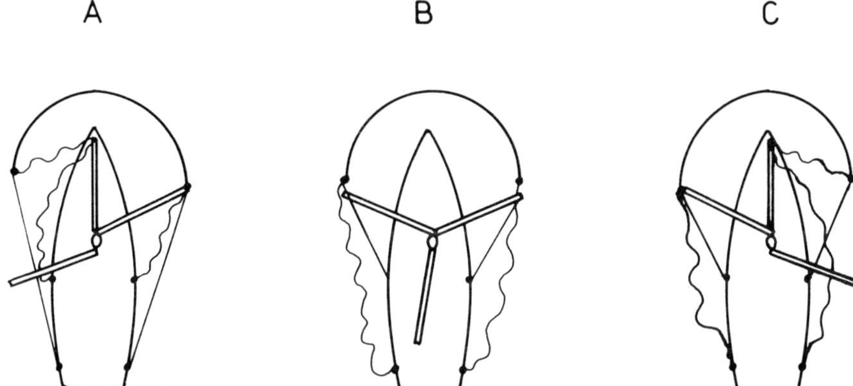

37. Double-pole gybe (double sheets and after guys or braces are essential). A: the second pole is set with outer end on foredeck, inner end connected to the mast at the required height; the port side lazy guy or brace is fitted into the pole end. B: the port pole is swung aft and raised to required height with the lazy guy or brace attached. Take port side load of spinnaker on the after guy that is running through the pole, release load on original port side sheet. C: take starboard side spinnaker load on lazy sheet and release load on old starboard side after guy. Lower pole forward on to foredeck with the old guy or brace attached. Release lazy after guy or brace from redundant starboard pole; you can now re-adjust the starboard side sheet to take load on whichever line is more convenient.

direction (see plate 48). With both of these systems, the pole is not removed from the mast during gybing. The fittings on the mast for the inner end of the pole are usually cup- or bayonet-type, as these fittings are stronger and more robust than the rings and therefore better suited to larger yacht application (see plates 49 and 50).

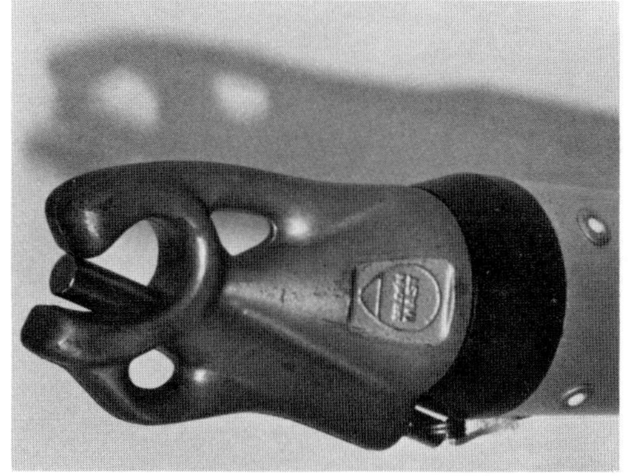

Plate 47. An end-opening spinnaker pole fitting. Note the shape of the aperture for the guy, and angle of the plunger, preventing accidental release of the guy. The plunger will also help to eject the old guy during a gybing operation.

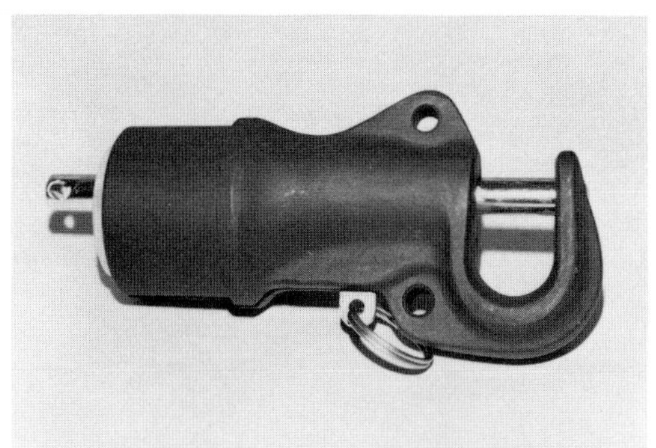

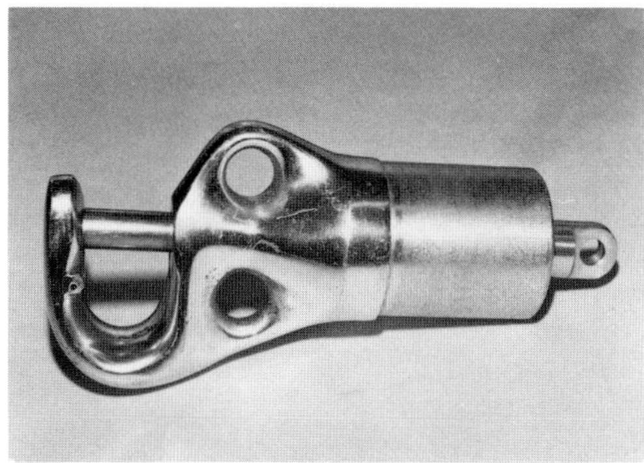

Plate 48. Top: a standard type of top-opening spinnaker pole and fitting. Bottom: a top-opening trip trigger end fitting: you can see the trip mechanism in the centre of the hook. As the plunger is withdrawn, the release trigger will rise in the hook and hold the plunger back (open). When downward pressure from the guy is applied to the release trigger, it will release the plunger over the guy.

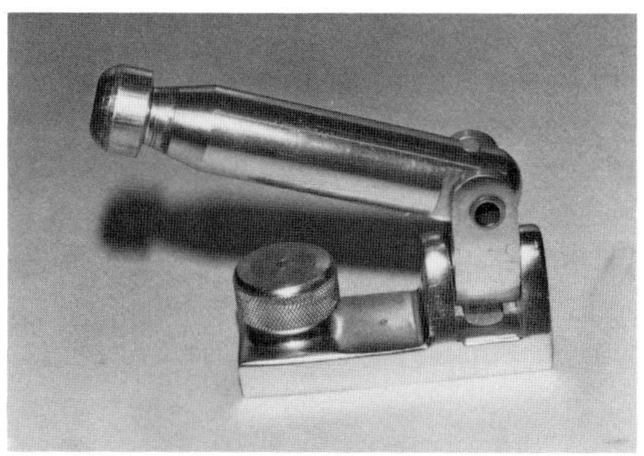

Plate 49. A bayonet-type slide for connecting the pole to the mast for double-pole or dip-pole gybing.

Maintenance

It is not usually possible to strip down spinnaker pole end fittings and, indeed, this should not be necessary, as all that is required is to keep them free from salt water crystallisation and frequently lubricated with light oil or an aerosol spray lubricant. Should a mechanical breakdown occur with these fittings, you would be well advised to return them to your spar maker for service or replacement.

Common Faults with Top-Opening Spinnaker Pole End Fittings

One of the biggest problems is the undesirable tendency of certain designs to open accident-

Plate 50. A cup and slide for connecting the spinnaker pole to the mast. It may be used with adjustable track stops, as illustrated, or with a heel lift/downhaul attached to the two vertical eyes. It is designed for use on yachts over 11 metres (36ft) overall length on dip-pole or double-pole gybing systems.

Plate 51. Shock cord fitted to top-opening pole, helping to prevent plunger opening and releasing guy.

ally when in use. This usually happens at the outer end because of the working of the guy through the pole end fittings. The guy manages to rotate the plunger and work it slowly open against the spring pressure, eventually releasing itself from the pole end. Pole end fittings which suffer most from this failing are the ones where the plunger assembly is able to rotate completely. Some plungers are not free to turn in this way and can only be withdrawn front to back; this is one way of overcoming this problem. Other designs have a separate roller on the plunger, so that the working of the guy just turns this roller. If you have a spinnaker pole end that has this problem, it may be possible to have a stronger spring fitted, but this will only be a temporary solution, as the spring may tire again. One do-it-yourself cure I have seen was the ingenious use of shock cord to give extra support to the spring. The owner who carried out this modification assured me that this overcame all his problems; plate 51 shows how it was rigged. It is worth noting that the end-opening pole cannot suffer in this way because the guy never works in an outward direction; even if it were possible for the plunger to be opened, the guy would still not leave the pole end.

Spinnaker Boom Mast Attachments

For cruising yachts up to 11 metres (36ft), a single fixed eye on the front of the mast is all that is required. This is because boats which do not race seldom carry more than one spinnaker, and they only use it when running dead down wind, or alternatively the pole may be used for booming out a genoa or headsail. Under these circumstances you will find that it is only necessary to have one position on the mast for the pole. On yachts of 7·5 metres overall (24ft 6in) this will be found to be about shoulder height, whereas yachts of about 11 metres overall length will have fixed rings a little above head height for the average man.

The spinnaker pole track and sliding eye principle has advantages for both cruising and racing boats. For the racing man, the advantage is that the inboard end of the pole can be readily adjusted so as to keep the spinnaker pole horizontal for whichever conditions prevail: the pole can be brought well down the mast for reaching, and set higher when running. If the track is continued to deck level, the spinnaker pole can be lowered to this point and left stowed along the foredeck. For the owner who does not wish to have his decks cluttered, the spinnaker track can serve as a useful alternative means of stowage. If this track is run further up the front of the mast, for at least the length of the pole, the ring can be hoisted to its maximum height so that the spinnaker pole can hang vertically from the ring. Suitable brackets are available for fitting to the bottom of the mast, so that the outer end of the pole can be secured (see plates 52 and 53). If it is not convenient to stow the pole down the front of the mast, because of through-mast reefing handles or winches which could be fouled by this arrangement, another possibility is to stow the pole vertically on one of the lower shrouds.

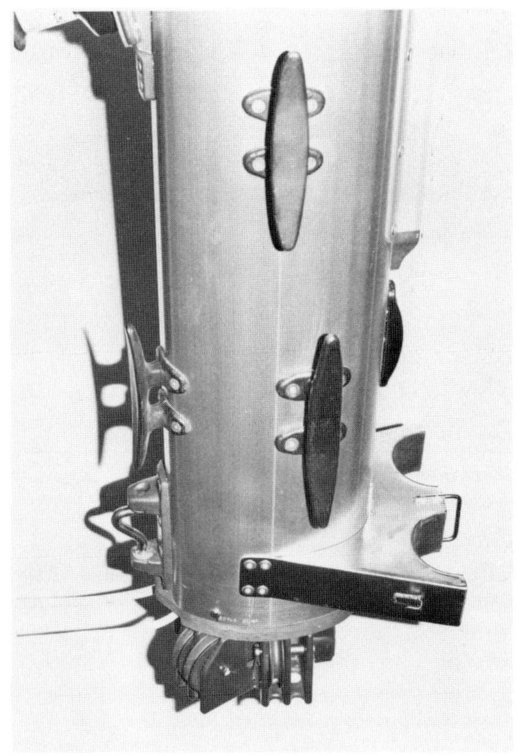

Plate 52. A double-pole stowage bracket for twin running sails on an 11 metre (36ft) cruising yacht.

Plate 53. Double spinnaker pole vertical stowage. Top: double stowage bracket. Middle: poles stowed. Note protection given to lower end of poles by up-stand on the deck. Bottom: upper end of double pole stowage.

Your spar maker will normally ensure that your spinnaker pole end fitting is compatible with the fitting on the mast. If you should decide to add a spinnaker pole or running sail boom at a later date, and your mast already has a ring or sliding eye fitted, you should take care that the pole you purchase will be compatible. Here there are two main problems. The first is to ensure that the ring diameter matches the end fitting (see below), and the second point is to ensure that the pole end fitting cannot lock in the ring when moved in any sailing position, and this includes skying of the pole when a crew member has accidentally released the downhaul or foreguy. Recapping on the first point, with so many different types of spinnaker pole end fittings available, there cannot possibly be one ring or fitting to cover all types of pole end fitting. Some have very narrow jaws and others are very wide. If one of the pole fittings with narrow jaws was paired with a large diameter ring, there would be nothing to keep it in the centre of this ring, and once the compression load came on the pole, it would move around until it locked and, when the load became too great, the end fitting itself would bend or break (see fig. 38). The ideal is a pole fitting that, because of its width, will be located in the centre of the ring, and will not be able to move off-centre far enough to cause the deflection loads as shown in the first example. The fitting should always bear on the outer surface of the ring (see fig. 38). However, a balance is required: if the end fitting is a good fit in the ring, it stops the deflection load, but care must be taken that it is still free to move in the vertical plane (see fig. 39).

The cup, slide and bayonet fittings do not have the same problems as the ring, for they both have universal joints, allowing freedom of movement in all directions. They are also a lot more expensive than the ring systems, and have the disadvantage of being suitable only for dip-pole or double-pole gybe systems. This is why there are few of these fittings

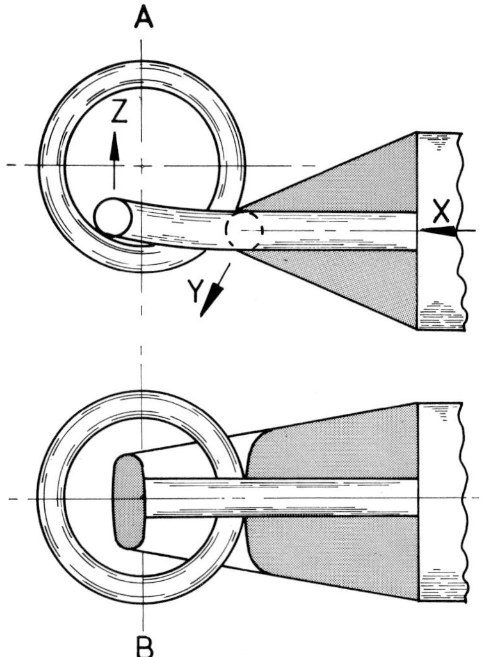

38. A: plan view of a slim spinnaker pole end fitted into a ring that is too large in diameter for it. When compression load X is applied, the end fitting will try and move round the ring in the direction of arrow Y. This results in a leverage on the end of the pole Z, with consequent bending or breaking of the spinnaker pole end fitting and/or the ring. B: a plan view of a wider design of spinnaker pole end fitting attached to the same diameter ring. Because of the width of the end fitting, it cannot move far enough off centre and cause the bending moment as in A. Note that the inner part of the hook of the spinnaker pole end fitting bears on the outer diameter of the ring.

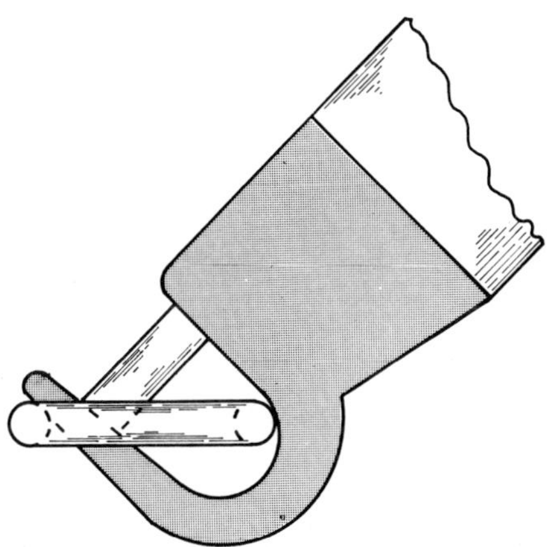

39. The spinnaker pole end fitting is not free to move vertically, and jams in the ring, causing bending of the ring and/or breakage of the spinnaker pole end fitting.

available for yachts of under 11 metres (36ft) overall (see plates 49 and 50).

Jockey Pole (Reaching Strut)

These are used when carrying a spinnaker on a shy reach. Their job is to deflect the spinnaker guy, for two reasons. First, it improves the angle at which the guy works and thus reduces the compression load in the pole, and secondly it prevents the spinnaker guy damaging the lifelines and stanchions. On most yachts where the shrouds are set in from the lifelines, the natural run of the guy will be from the end of the spinnaker pole to the point on the boat where the block is attached, which will generally be aft of the yacht's maximum beam, and you can see from figure 40 that the guy then passes over the lifelines; the jockey pole keeps it clear. It is attached to the mast by means of an eye plate fastened to the side rather than the front of the mast. The height of this eye is not critical, and it should be positioned to suit the height of the spinnaker pole, which depends on the type of spinnaker in use. If, as is likely, it is a flat cut reacher, the spinnaker pole will be set just above the pulpit, and in this case the jockey pole, likewise, needs to be positioned well down the mast; the limiting factor will generally be the height of the lifelines, as the jockey pole will rest on these wires when deflecting the guy. It is possible, if a slightly fuller spinnaker is being used on a shy reach, that it will not be necessary for the spinnaker pole to be positioned as low as mentioned above. If it is higher, then similarly the jockey pole eye plate will have to be raised to the level of the guy when it is immediately adjacent to the mast. The jockey pole is set by first attaching the inner end to the mast, and the pole is swung forward so that the outer end sheave connects with the guy. The pole is then forced aft, deflecting the guy outboard until the jockey pole comes up against the lower shroud. At this point, it should be

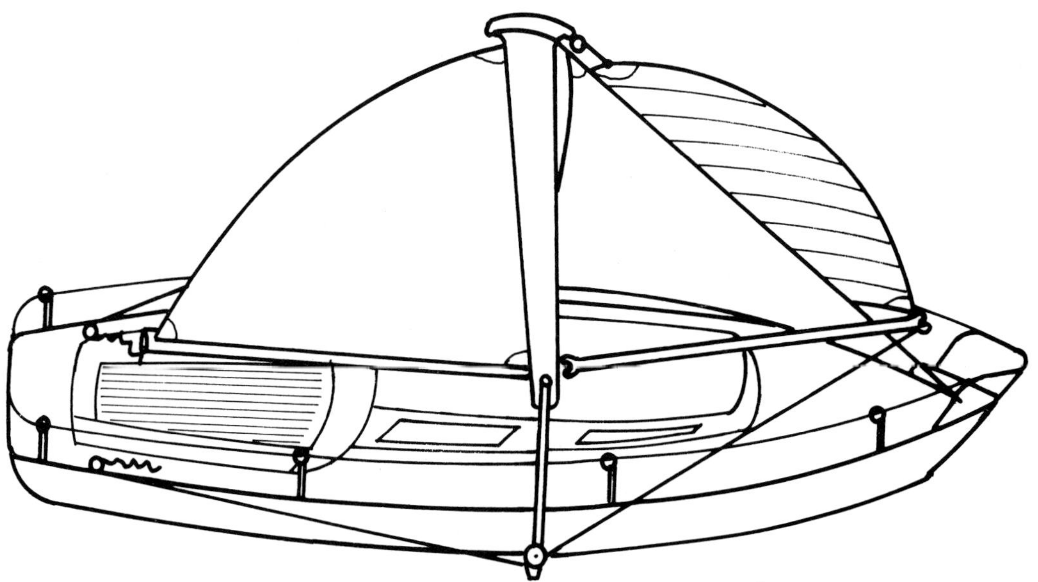

40. The jockey pole or reaching strut deflects the spinnaker after guy or brace and keeps it away from the stanchions and life lines. It also improves the angle between guy and pole, giving better control of the spinnaker pole and reducing load in both brace and pole.

lashed to the shroud to prevent it from moving when adjustment is made on the spinnaker guy. If it is more convenient, it can be fitted in the reverse direction, i.e. swung aft first then forced forward (see plate 54).

Maintenance

This is the same as for spinnaker poles: just keep the moving parts of the outboard sheave and inboard plunger free of salt water crystallisation, and lubricate regularly with light oil or aerosol lubricant.

Plate 54. A Three-Quarter Tonner on a broad spinnaker reach. Note the use of the jockey pole to hold the spinnaker guy off the shroud and so give more control to the spinnaker pole. Photo: John Etches.

ten

Other Types of Rig

Up to this point I have generalised on fittings and their uses for all types of mast, but have only discussed the staying and rigs of the single-spreader masthead arrangement, either deck- or keel-stepped. It is therefore appropriate to finish with a chapter on the merits and tuning of double-spreader and fractional rigs.

Double-Spreader Masthead Rig

The advantage of this rig is that it gives additional side support by splitting the column length into three parts instead of two. This means that the mast section can be reduced without any loss of safety factors.

Double-spreader rigs are commonly used on cutter-rigged boats. This is because the attachment of the inner forestay is required to be two-thirds up the mast to give a decent-sized staysail, and the upper spreaders are ideally placed to give the required side support for this stay. On high aspect ratio rigs, the length of spreaders and chain plate width is reduced without any loss of shroud angle. This means that the genoa can be sheeted in closer. On narrow-beamed boats, such as the old six metres, where it is impossible to fit chain plates far enough out from the mast for a single-spreader rig, a double-spreader has to be used. These are the principal advantages of a double-spreader rig; there are, of course, disadvantages. Firstly, there is more standing rigging which makes tuning of the spars slightly more difficult than that of a single-spreader rig. Secondly, as can be seen from figure 41, the lower spreaders, and consequently the lower shrouds, are much further down the mast. This means that fore and aft support is kept to the lower height, leaving no support between this point and the mast head. This in itself is not a great problem, providing the owner is prepared to use runners during certain wind strengths and sea states. Maybe the use of the word 'runners' in this context is bad, as it implies the necessity for a permanently-rigged stay, which needs constant adjustment when tacking and gybing. This is not so. Perhaps the word preventer would be more appropriate; under average conditions it will not be necessary to use such a stay. However, in choppy, steep waves and when the main is reefed, the mast at the upper spreader could start panting, or working in a fore and aft direction. It is at this time that it would be advisable to have a light preventer to be attached to a block and tackle, brought aft to a suitable strong point on the toe rail or genoa track. The loads on these preventers will be light, and can be taken up on a three- or four-part handy billy.

For ease of tuning the side rigging, it is recommended that the intermediate shrouds as well as the caps be led down to the chain plates. When setting up this rig, both these shrouds will need constant adjustment until the mast is tuned and correct. Linking them at the lower spreader means that a crew

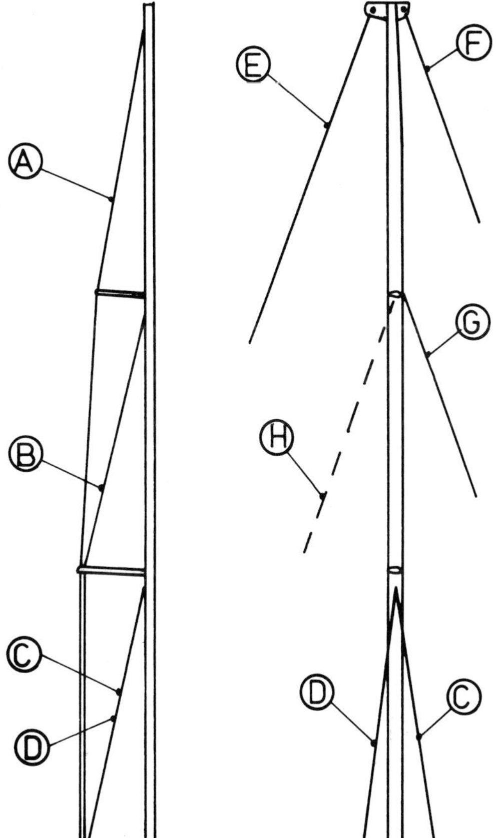

41. Double-spreader rig. A: cap shroud clamped to upper spreader, but running freely through the tip of the lower spreader. B: intermediate shroud clamped to lower spreader and led to chain plate. C: forward lower shroud. D: aft lower shroud. E: backstay. F: forestay. G: inner forestay (used with cutter rigs). H: preventers. A double-spreader rig will have 9 to 10 per cent narrower chain plate beam than a single-spreader rig of the same mast height.

member has to go aloft and undo tape and split pins, adjust the rigging screw, lock it off, and repeat the sailing trials to see what difference this has made. This may have to be carried out two or three times before the rig is satisfactorily tuned. By keeping these rigging screws at deck level, tuning is made far easier.

It is just as important with double spreaders as with single spreaders to have them locked on to the shrouds. The upper spreader is obviously clamped securely to the cap shroud, but the lower should be clamped securely to the intermediate shroud, not to the cap shroud. The intermediate shroud is the one that is angled around the spreader end, and the cap shroud is hardly deflected at all, so all the compression load on the lower spreader comes from the intermediate.

Fractional Rigs

Fractional rigs are not new, and have proved themselves over the years, providing they are correctly engineered. In the pursuit of speed, however, masts have been tapered, jumpers have been eliminated and weight cut down until overmuch reliance has to be placed on running backstays and preventers. One mistake in crew drill can lose the rig. Three-quarter or seven-eighths rigs do, however, have certain advantages for the out-and-out racing enthusiast (but the cruising man should beware of such a boat if he should be

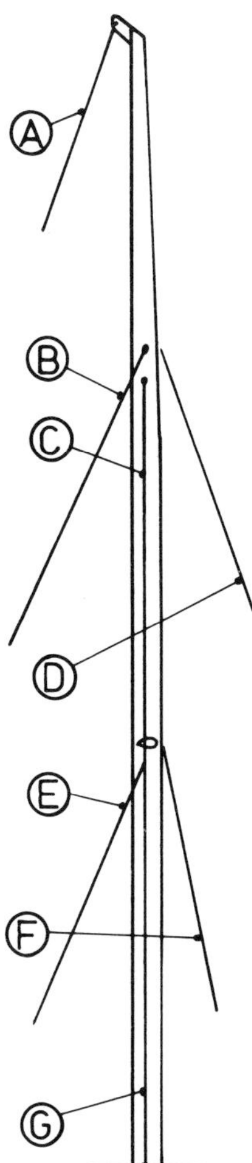

tempted into buying one secondhand; they take a lot of expertise). The genoa may be carried in a greater range of wind strengths, through bending the mast to flatten the mainsail, and also twisting the sail to allow the leech to spill wind. Often the top of the sail is completely feathered down the line of the air stream. As the wind increases and decreases, the top of the mast must flex to allow the leech to twist in the gusts and tighten in the lulls so as to keep the maximum usable power throughout the greater wind strength range, thus obviating the need and loss of time for headsail changes.

The type of rig described above is shown in figure 42. Note that the lowers are in line with the main cap shrouds. If they were raked aft, they would prevent the mast bending and flattening the mainsail. To allow the mainsail to work efficiently, the top of the mast has to be reduced in section considerably (tapered). A large topmast section would cause more turbulence on the reduced mainsail chord length, therefore only a small percentage of the mainsail would be working efficiently. Let us take a hypothetical example.

A mast causes turbulence on the lee side of the mainsail for up to 500mm (20in). The mainsail at this point has a chord length of 4 metres (13ft); this means that eighty-five to ninety per cent of the mainsail is working effectively in the clean air stream. If the same size of mast were above the hounds and the mainsail at this point had a chord length of 1 metre (3ft 3in), only fifty per cent of the sail

42. Fractional rig for racing yachts. A: backstay (used for bend control only). B: running backstay (for supporting forestay). C: cap shrouds. D: forestay. E: lower preventers (used for bend control). F: babystay. G: lower shrouds. This type of rig, having cap shrouds and lower shrouds on the athwartships mast centre line, must have runners and preventers. If runners and preventers were omitted, the rig would have only the backstay trying to hold the mast in the boat, a task it will not perform because of the smallness of the mast section at the top.

would be working in clean air. Above the point where the chord length was 500mm, that part of the sail would be in wholly turbulent airstream. So from this example it can be seen that the mast section must be tapered to give the top of the mainsail a chance to work properly. At this point you may well say that the same is true for a masthead rig. However, you cannot taper a masthead rig section because of the compression loadings imposed by the large genoas. In addition, the mainsail is a smaller percentage of the sail area on a masthead rig, and you are therefore only losing efficiency on a smaller percentage of the total sail area.

Returning to our fractional rig with a tapered top section on the mast, look again at the drawing. You have a backstay that is attached to the top of a thin mast head. This can only really be used to bend the top of this rig; it cannot give any fore and aft support–the weakness of the top section precludes this. Coming down the mast, there are runners which oppose the loads imposed by the genoa and the forestay. These have to be made up on the weather side, slackened on tacking, and the ones on the new weather side made up. Further down the mast are preventers. Because there are no aft lowers, preventers are essential to control the amount of bend put in the mast. Without them, the compression loading in the lower part of the rig would cause the mast to buckle once it came out of a straight vertical line. From this description you can see that there could be a time when there is very little holding the mast up and preventing it from going over the bow of the yacht if it is deck-stepped, or breaking off at deck level if it is keel-stepped. This is exactly what can–and does–happen with these rigs occasionally. They are purely for racing, and require a crew on board who know how to use them. Runners, preventers and backstays are adjustable, and have to be worked at continually to get the best out of the rig, and to keep it in the boat. They are certainly not a practical proposition for cruising.

Fractional Rigs for Cruisers and Cruiser/Racers

Despite the above, more and more cruising yachts are appearing with fractional rigs, and I wish to point out how misguided a compromise between the racing and cruising rigs can be. I believe that these rigs have been bred for this category of boat out of fashion rather than logic.

The main advantage of a fractional rig for a cruising boat is that the small genoa can be handled with smaller winches and, with improved reefing and handling systems for the mainsail, the big main is easier to control, thus making it a good arrangement for the family cruising man and helping him to club race with the current race-winning style of rig. To obtain these features and to overcome the handling problems of runners and preventers, rigs have been developed with spreaders which are swept aft twenty-five to thirty degrees in plan view, with the chain-plates to suit (see fig. 43). With this system, you should not require runners or preventers, as the lowers must be taken aft to the same chainplates as the cap shrouds. This type of rig can be seen on several designs on the water today; it is safe and will work. But how well does it work, and would these boats not be faster with masthead rig and as easy to handle? When considering the following points we must completely discount the out-and-out racing three-quarter rig. There have been many trials over recent years, and there is a lot of evidence to support the masthead rig. I, for one, believe that this type of three-quarter rig is a poor compromise, with the disadvantages of both fractional and mast-head racing rigs, and the advantages of neither. I believe that these yachts, equipped with masthead rigs, would be just as easy to handle and would give far better performance in club racing. This I believe for the following reasons.

The mast bend cannot be controlled, as the spreaders and lowers prevent change of mast shape to suit the mainsail, and restrict the total amount of bend possible with this type of rig.

The forestay is only supported by the tension in the cap shrouds which act at a maximum of 6° from the vertical when the spreaders are swept aft 30°.

The forestay can never be kept tight,

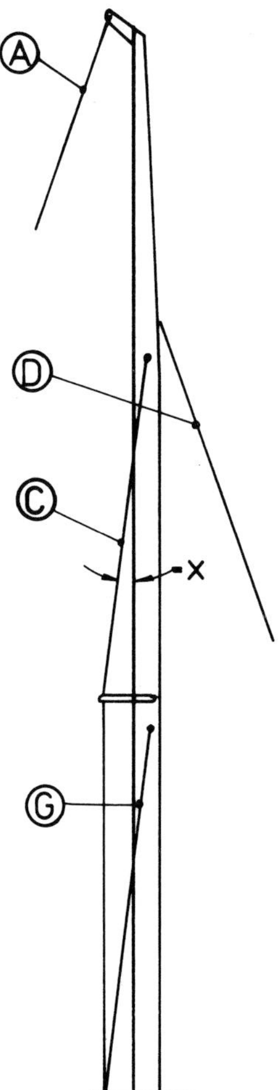

43. Fractional rig for cruiser and cruiser/racer. A: backstay (used for bend control only). C: cap shrouds with backstay angle X of about 6°. D: forestay. G: aft-angled lower shrouds. With this type of rig, all the forestay tension is taken on the cap shrouds C, which only gives a vertical support angle X of 6° when the spreaders and chain plates are angled 30° aft from the athwartships centre line (viewed from above). The backstay is too far from the forestay to have any effect on the forestay tension.

though this is the first requirement for efficient windward sailing, because of the poor backstay support. The forestay carries only a quarter to a third of the cap shroud load (on a masthead rig, forestay tension is higher than backstay tension because the backstay is at a wider angle to the mast).

Remember high load means a large amount of stretch (see Chapter 3). The cap shrouds, because of their poor working angle, are subject to very high loads in an attempt to keep some semblance of tension in the forestay. As the cap shrouds carry two or three times the forestay load they have high stretch, e.g. a forestay height above deck of about 9500mm may allow the shrouds to stretch 20mm. Due to the cap shrouds poor aft angle this 20mm of stretch allows the mast at forestay attachment point to move diagonally forward 290mm. This movement of the mast puts approximately 370mm of leeward sag in the forestay. The forestay itself will stretch; this plus the lowering effect of the mast forestay attachment point, due to mast bend, will give forestay sag of over 400mm, and there is nothing you can do to control this effect. (See fig. 44).

The figures above are given for the stretch that is likely to occur in one wind strength; regrettably this figure changes constantly with the wind and sea state. As the wind increases, forestay sag increases, and there is no way to control it or prevent it from happening, which is entirely the opposite from what you require. The hollow that your sail maker cuts in the luff of the genoa will be correct for one condition of forestay sag, i.e. your genoa will be perfect in 10 knots of wind, but on strengths above this the forestay will sag, the genoa will get fuller and the yacht will be rapidly overpowered and lose pointing ability, and in wind strengths of less than 10 knots the forestay sag will be less, which will flatten the genoa and reduce power, again the reverse effect to that which you require in the lighter wind strengths.

With the 30° aft sweep on spreaders and chain plates, the boom will be prevented from being squared off, as it will be restricted by the cap shrouds. This has three main disadvantages: the large main cannot be let right out when running dead down wind; the spreaders will cause bad creases and puckers in the mainsail, and this in turn will cause excessive chafe; finally, when broad reaching, a broach cannot be forestalled by freeing off the mainsail so easily, because it can only be released to 60° from the fore and aft line.

With any three-quarter rig, you must have your mainsail working effectively when running or broad reaching, to compensate for the small spinnaker. The main problem appears to be the inability to control forestay sag, so the obvious answer would seem to be to use runners when club racing and suffer the detrimental features when cruising with the family; after all, performance is not so important when cruising, but ease of handling is. This, on the face of it, sounds like a good solution, but it is not that simple. If you use

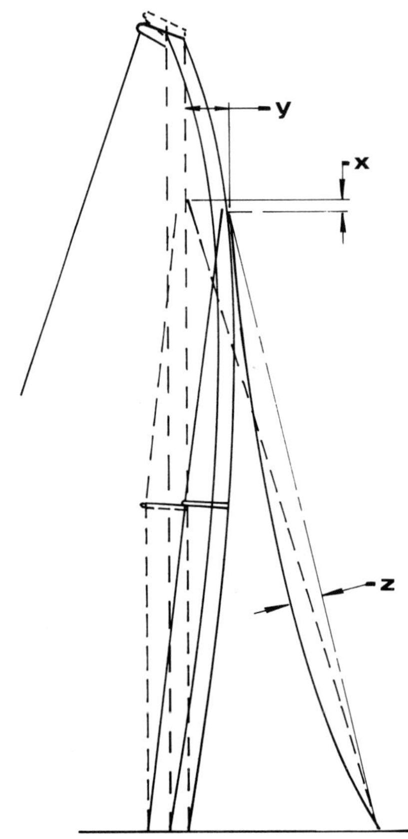

44. This picture shows the exaggerated effect of stretch in cap shrouds. Y: the forward movement of the mast due to the stretch in the shrouds. X: the height reduction of the forestay attachment due to mast bend. Z: forestay sag.

runners to tension the forestay, you pull the hounds aft and immediately slacken the aft swept cap shrouds, and consequently lose athwartships control and mast stability, making the mast difficult if not impossible to tune, causing some alarming shapes when sailing to windward.

To sum up, the main disadvantages of this rig are:

1. Lack of control of mast bend and mainsail shape.
2. Increased shroud load and mast compression.
3. Lack of control of genoa shape.
4. Restriction of main downwind and mainsail wear.
5. Considerable forestay sag.

The advantages are:

1. Small genoa for ease of handling.
2. Large powerful mainsail.
3. Small spinnaker.

I believe that the advantages of this type of rig are outweighed by the disadvantages in operation. With a masthead rig, the main disadvantage is the handling of large headsails, but you can at least control forestay tension and headsail shape, thus keeping the rig efficient when racing, and when cruising you can always set a smaller headsail for ease of handling, or use a roller-reefing forestay.

It is therefore my opinion that there is no compromise; you either race and have a flat-out three-quarter rig with runners, preventers and a team of experts to handle them, or you have a good old conventional masthead rig. There is no middle road, as a fashionable three-quarter rig will not make you go faster if it is just for appearance: it has to be used correctly. The masthead rig may not look as trendy but it will be easy to use and control. Sail area for sail area, the masthead rig is more efficient than the aft-swept shroud three-quarter rig, although, properly handled, the most efficient rig of all is probably the no-compromise squared-off spreader three-quarter rig for racing boats, as described earlier in the chapter.

eleven

Annual Maintenance and Halyard Replacement

Annual Maintenance

It is advisable to remove the mast from the boat every winter, so that the annual inspection and maintenance may be properly carried out.

When the rig is off the boat, all halyards, especially the parts which run inside the mast and are therefore not normally visible, should be carefully checked. Normally this can be done without taking the halyards out of the mast, but should it be necessary to remove them, they should be replaced by a thin nylon messenger line for ease of re-reeving. If you find any abnormal chafes and abrasions, the cause should be found and remedied. All ropes and lines should be carefully washed in fresh water and dried; shackles and spinnaker end fittings should be washed, dried and lightly oiled.

The alloy spars themselves should be washed off with fresh water, so that all salt crystals are removed. It may be necessary to use warm, soapy water, although detergents should be avoided: they often contain substances which can cause corrosion in the alloy (use a fairly expensive hand soap–when your wife is not looking). Pay particular attention to the base of the mast, where it is most likely to corrode, through salt water lying there. Do not forget to flush out the inside of the mast, as the anodising is at its least effective here. The mast must be thoroughly dried so that all traces of soap and water are removed. Lightly oil all moving parts, and silicone wax polish the mast, luff tracks and spinnaker tracks. It is important that the mast and boom are dry and clean before they are eventually packed away for the winter. Never put spars in a plastic bag or other air tight container before they are carefully cleaned and dried in accordance with the above instructions.

Re-running Halyards when the Mast is Stepped

We have already discussed winter maintenance, which incorporates the removal of fittings and halyards and their re-running. It is however possible that halyards will be broken or lost inside the mast during the sailing season, or that you will want to add additional internal halyards when it is inconvenient to remove the mast from the boat. Therefore methods have to be found to run or re-run them. The main problem is to ensure that the halyard goes down inside the mast without twisting round other halyards or internal mast fittings.

Make sure that all other internal halyards are made off as tightly as possible. Go aloft to the entry of the halyard in question, taking with you a small link chain which is about 300mm (1ft) long, and of suitable size to pass over the sheave. Also, have available a thin messenger line of the size you would use on your burgee halyard. Attach this line to the chain, and you are now ready to run the messenger through the mast. If the lower halyard exit is on the starboard side of the mast, get one of your crew to stand on the starboard side of the boat to heel the yacht so that, when the messenger line is dropped down inside, it will follow the starboard mast wall and will not spiral round any other halyards or fittings on the way down. If the lower exit box is removable, it will make life easier if it is taken off the mast. If the exit sheave is in the heel fitting, and therefore the complete box cannot be removed, just remove the appropriate sheave.

Run the chain down the mast slowly until it is visible through the opening left by the exit box or sheave. With a bent piece of wire, you should catch the chain and pull it through the spare opening. Then you can run it through the correct exit box which is held away from the mast. You have now got a complete messenger run in place of the halyard; the person aloft should attach the rope tail of the halyard to the messenger, and gently feed it into the mast through the upper sheave position. Carefully pull the halyard down through the mast until the messenger is completely replaced by the halyard. You can now replace the appropriate sheave or exit box.

appendix
Tools and Spares and Mast vibration

Tools and Spares

Screw Driver–Medium for self-tapping screws size 8 to 12.

Screw Driver–Small (electrical) for the electrical terminals in the mast lights.

Adjustable Spanner–Medium for tensioning shroud tang bolts and headbox securing bolts.

Pliers–Medium for opening up and removing split pins.

Hand Drill–Chuck capacity up to (1/4in) or 6·5mm. This is better than a 12 volt electric drill, as there are jobs where it may be necessary to go aloft where a power supply would be difficult to organise.

Set of Twist Drills–Maximum size (1/4in) or 6·5mm diameter.

Hack Saw–Junior type may be easiest to store in the kit.

Vice–Small Portable type for holding fittings that may require adjustment, or screws and bolts that may need shortening. At least have a pair of Mole Grips if a vice is impractical.

Hammer (ball peen) I am sure we can all think of a good use for this universal tool.

Rivet Tongs this is probably the most useful tool, but one of the most difficult to obtain in the required size range. 5mm (3/16in) maximum riveting pliers are widely obtainable, but these will only cover a small part of your requirements; a tool that can expand the 6·5mm (1/4in) diameter nickel copper alloy (trade name Monel), is essential, and until recently has been a rare tool outside boatyards and rigging specialists. Be careful not to be sold a 6·5mm (1/4in) rivetting tong that will only expand aluminium rivets, as these rivets can be expanded by a much lighter tool than that required to expand monel rivets. The type of rivet tool suitable is rarely sold at chandlers or Do-It-Yourself centres. One of the few retail stockists are Kemp Masts Ltd, St. Margarets Lane, Titchfield, Fareham, Hants, England. In 1979 they sold them for about £30.00+VAT, and they are worth every penny. I make no apology for this advertising as there is no point in my recommending this tool if the reader cannot readily find a supplier. The rivet tool obtained from the above supplier can be bought with interchangeable nozzles that will cover most sizes of rivets.

Rivets keep small stocks of various lengths of rivet in 6·5mm (1/4in) and 5mm (3/16in) diameter. These can be obtained fairly easily in alloy but are almost impossible to find in monel–I can only recommend Kemp Masts Ltd at address given above, or probably your local mast maker may sell you a few.

Bosun's Chair The polyester and webbing construction chairs are probably the safest, as you are securely held in them and have freedom of movement to climb (to assist your winch winder) and adjust your position without the chance of coming out of the chair. These chairs have a centre webbing which passes between your legs and another that passes round your waist, and these connect at a front ring on to which the halyard is attached. There is also, on most types, an eye on the underside of the chair to which a downhaul is attached so as to stop you swinging round when on an exposed mooring or at sea. It also has useful pockets for carrying tools and fittings. The only problem with this type of bosun's chair is that it can be very restricting if you have to be aloft for any length of time.

The other type of bosun's chair which overcomes the discomforts for long periods is the wooden seat type, which is not so safe to use. For the odd job of maintenance aloft stay with the polyester type, they are much safer. Remember, never walk below anyone working aloft–even the most skilled rigger can drop tools or fittings.

Self-Tapping Screws (stainless steel only) these are always useful standbys, not only for quick spar jobs but also for numerous uses around the yacht.

Whipping Twine (polyester) used for re-running halyards (see Chapter 11) also useful for whipping halyard tails for that really professional look.

Chain–Small link of a size that will easily pass over the masthead sheaves, and of any stock length, but not less than 100mm (4in). This is attached to the whipping twine for re-running halyards (see Chapter 11).

Split Pins (assorted stainless steel) never use brass, as there could be danger of electrolytic action if close to aluminium. Carry spares of the size used in rigging screws and mast tangs particularly.

Tape (*PVC*) for covering all split pins, spreader ends, rigging screws, toggles and insulating electrical wiring.

Grease, water repellant, of the type used in stern tube and water circulating pumps, for use on winches and worm reefing gear.

Light Oil as an alternative to the aerosol lubricant.

Aerosol Lubricant the cleanest and easiest general purpose lubricant.

Silicone Rubber (tube of) used for sealing round deck level mast coats, on keel stepped masts, particularly in the track or groove area.

Files (various) useful to keep six or so different grades of coarseness, size and shape.

Shackles keep a duplicate of all the types used that are not secured permanently on wire, rope or fittings.

Bolt Croppers these are not essential for coastal work, but anyone thinking of longer trips would be well advised to carry them. The most experienced seaman can lose a rig through one of many reasons: when it does happen, conditions are usually bad, and a broken mast in a heavy sea can cause a lot of damage. Bolt croppers are the quickest and easiest method of cutting away the rigging to either jettison the mast or help to untangle the rigging.

Bulldog or U Grips at least two for each size of wire on the yacht, to help you to sail home if you are having problems with rigging in an area where professional help is not available.

Rigging Wire one spare length for replacing a damaged stay. By using bulldog grips, you can make it up to suit the stay length that is required, thus reducing the number and length of wires carried.

Swageless Terminal (Norseman, Sta-lock or Electroline) a spare for each size of rigging wire will give a stronger, neater and quicker repair than the bulldog grips. They are, however, more expensive.

Mast vibration

This is an effect that can occur on any mast, particularly deck stepped masts and masts with poor lower fore and aft staying. Mast vibration causes a lot of noise inside the yacht and is very disturbing at night, so anything that can be done to reduce the effect will be beneficial.

1. Theory

Vibration appears at moderate windspeeds, approximately 2–6metres/second (5–14 miles per hour), and the mast theoretically oscillates in a direction perpendicular to the wind. In practice, however, nearly all vibration occurs in an athwartships wind direction. The oscillations are caused by alternate eddy shedding on the lee side of the mast and the frequency depends on windspeed, mast section size and shape.

When the natural frequency of the mast coincides with the frequency of oscillation, resonance is said to occur, the amplitude suddenly increases to a maximum and severe vibration appears. The lower the windspeed at which resonance occurs, the smaller the amplitude of vibration. The amplitude depends greatly on the size of the section, and the mechanical and aerodynamic damping are also important.

Despite its great technical importance the "Karman" effect still contains many uncertain details, not only for yacht masts, but also for chimneys. Vibrations occur in all struts or columns of a high slenderness ratio but the particular amplitude and wind force can be affected in several ways.

2. Actions to minimise vibration

The mast section must be as small as possible in the longitudinal axis and increased section weight can also give a smaller vibration amplitude. It is possible to reduce vibration, possibly to an acceptable level with extra fore and aft staying. For example, a rod or wire inner forestay can be fitted. Any extra staying must be rod or wire to make any improvement, as polyester rope has too much stretch.

A more convenient cure for the problem is to hoist a stiff 9 oz. narrow strip (at least 100mm. wide) of sailcloth in the mast groove.

The vortex "streets" that are produced on the downwind side of the mast are separated, and the random turbulence into which these vortices break causing the vibration, is prevented.

3. Actions to change the resonant windspeed
Increasing the axial (compression) load on the mast, by tightening the stays, can decrease the natural frequency of the mast and therefore decrease the windspeed at which resonance occurs. Thus the resulting amplitude of oscillation is reduced.

4. Actions to decrease the disturbing effect
Internal halliards and cables can magnify the noise of vibration, but this source can be removed by using internal "cushions" made of polyurethane foam. Cables should be glued or wedged into the sail groove.

Index